Typographical Tourists

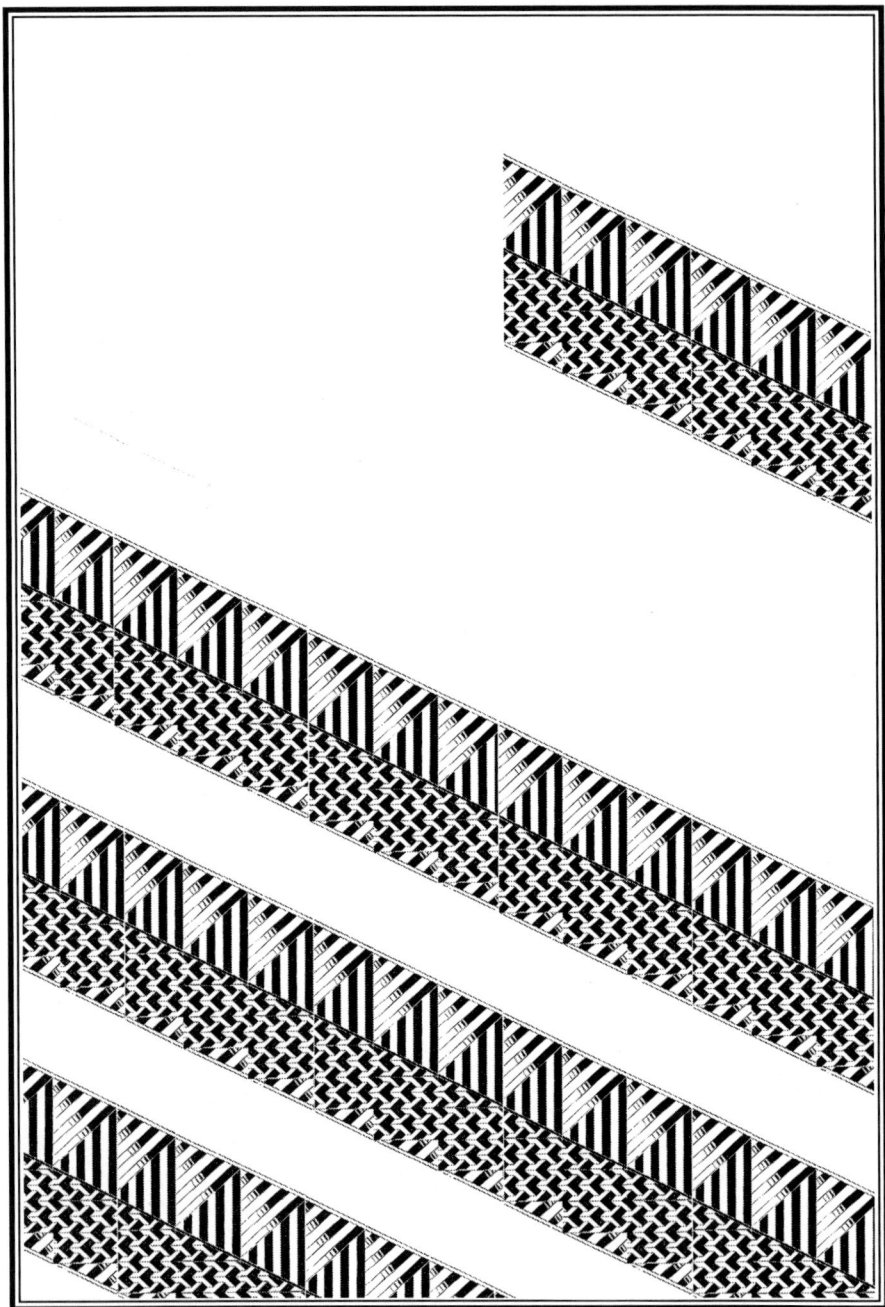

Typographical Tourists:

Tales of the Tramping Printer.

Edited by Alastair "EmQuad" Johnston

Poltroon Press
2012

ACKNOWLEDGMENTS

Thanks to Frances Butler, Tinker Greene, Bob Hirst (Director of the Mark Twain Project at UC Berkeley's Bancroft Library), and the Librarians of the California Historical Society, San Francisco. The periodical selections were found in the Kemble Collection of the California Historical Society, the Library of Congress' Historical American Newspapers collection, or in the Poltroon Press library.

ISBN: 0–918395–29–1

Printed in the USA by BookMobile for POLTROON PRESS,
P. O. Box 5476, Berkeley, CA 94705–0476

See the Tramp
Winks his Eye
& hies East

— Cleveland Type Foundry, 1893

Contents

A Big,
Phat
Take

YOU MAY GO from Madagascar to the confines of Alaska,
From the balmy western shore to where Atlantic's waters break—
Though you be a perfect stranger, you will never be in danger
Of mistaking who's the printer with a
   Big,
     Phat
       Take.

I have seen the smile ecstatic play on countenance Falstaffic
When an unexpected tipple came his parching thirst to slake,
But for pleasure unabated, pure and unadulterated,
Commend me to the typo with a
   Big,
     Phat
       Take.

You can never "chew the rag" on any printer with a "jag" on
(Though you use your best endeavors the poor derelict to "shake")
Without hearing the old story of the fortune and the glory
Of the fellow in his office with a
   Big,
     Phat
       Take.

— D. T. B.
 San Francisco, August 23, 1890.

Phat is the printers' term for copy with a lot of "air" or blank space in it, such as
poetry, which is consequently easier and quicker to typeset.

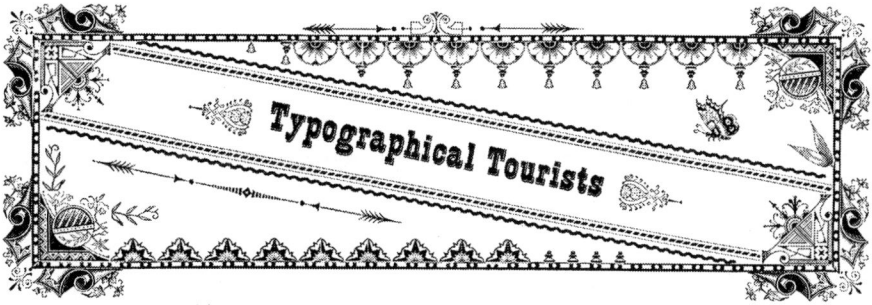

RESORTING TO INTOXICANTS to drive away despair, the best of compositors are themselves driven away to give place to men not unfitted for duty at the case by intemperate habits.

Why despair? Wherefor intemperance? Let me briefly sketch the checkered career of a typical tramp printer. From the time, as a lad, he first takes a stick into his hand, and carefully and slowly adjusts the type, his story is an interesting one.

He adopts the profession, perhaps, out of the same reason that thousands of others do. Its advantages are pointed out to him as a profession that is not alone remunerative, but educational; he admires the beauty of the mechanism of printing; and office-life seems highly desirable in contrast with outdoor labor, where wind, rain, and snow are to be contended with, and printing offices seem so nice and cosy. Everyone in country towns, save alone the printers themselves, are extolling the virtues of the business and envying the compositors.

So BEGINS F. MARION COLE in "A Plea for the Tramp Printer," written for the *Inland Printer* of Chicago at the close of the nineteenth century. But, Cole tells us, after several years the compositor ("comp") begins to think the cosy printshop is not so healthy: the chemicals are toxic, and so, to counteract the effects of ink, solvents, lead type and dust on his constitution, he fortifies it with John Barleycorn. Laboring on his feet all day under gas light he longs for the fresh air outdoors.

Thomas MacKellar wrote about this condition in his poem, "The Doom of the Printer":

> For twenty sad years and more,
> My life has worn away
> In murky rooms of poisonous air,
> When I've yearned for a sight of the valley fair
> And the light of open day.[1]

The great observer Charles Dickens (in his capacity as chairman of the Printers' Pension Corporation) noticed the pallor:

> Immured as he is, in a close confined place of business, from an early to a late hour, and frequently throughout the night, breathing little else than a tainted atmosphere, it is no wonder that he displays a cadaverous countenance and emaciated appearance.[2]

According to Jerry B. Graham, this explains his evil habits:

> No one familiar with the routine of a morning daily marveled at the proverbial dissipation of the old-time printer. He came from under the hot gas-light in the morning, exhausted and pale as a church bedbug. No wonder his coppers got hot pretty often. He needed rest, but was prone to substitute stimulants and forget the downy couch.[3]

Under the influence of "budge," the "jour" (journeyman) becomes a poor worker and is shown the door; thus begins a life on the road, interrupted by "sits" (situations), where he puts his name on the sub board of an unfamiliar city and tries to show his former skill as an ace compositor. If you held a "sit" long enough you might be honored to be called by your rank on the sub board, as we shall see when we meet Slugs 9, 11 and 14.

These men were educated, bold and carefree:

> They are the true Bohemians of the printing art, and for the most part lead a nomadic life. "Here to-day and gone to-morrow," is the motto necessity has inscribed upon their banner.* Many of them would prefer it otherwise; but the fluctuating condition of things

---

* "To 'carry the banner' means to walk the streets all night." – Jack London

will not permit, and at varying intervals they must move on, or policeman Short will arrest them and confiscate their often scanty wardrobe.

But a jollier set never carried the carpet-bag. Their happy-go-lucky manner is an infection, and they are too improvident ever to think of the rainy day. With willing hands and nimble fingers, a liberal profession at their command, and the scantiest kit — a bodkin or tweezers, and perhaps a stick — they know the world is before them, and are fearless of its terrors.[4]

The tramp printer was a proud, skilled craftsman who chose an uncertain bed and life on the road over a permanent situation. If, later in life, he gave in to alcoholism, it was to mask his shattered dreams.

By the 1890s the lore of the tramp printer began to appear in the trade periodicals. Though romanticized he could also be a real danger, as a letter to the editor of the *Inland Printer* attests:

AN IMPOSTOR

To the Editor: Appleton, Wis., September 28, 1889

One J. E. Bayard recently worked the printers in this vicinity for quite an amount. He does the write-up act. He collects as much as he can while doing the work and disappears like the dew before the morning sun. He is a smooth-faced, short, thick-set fellow, and seems lacking in honesty. He also neglects to pay his board bills. It might be a good thing to warn the fraternity against trusting him in any way: especially if he opens up any advertising scheme to the country publisher. Yours truly,

J. R.

The *Inland Printer* celebrated him in prose and verse, usually doggerel, such as

> *Good mornin' boys, and how is biz? I'm a seedy-looking tramp.*
> *You see, last night my little bed was just a trifle damp...*

After burbling a bit he comes to the punning part for his pie-eyed pious finish:

I've made some justification in this ancient, battered form;
My benzine wash I've thrown aside, it has brought me too much harm;
My proof has been corrected — a revise will needed be,
For He who searches every heart will many errors see.

A "devil" writing in the same paper predicts his own career trajectory:

> The career of the devil is shapen by himself. He may be a successful printer, a renowned author or editor, or a drunken sot of a tramp, a disgrace to the art; a knavish fool and a foolish knave. His course is made sure by the early commencement of reading cheap literature, familiarly called "dime novels," and acquiring the art of using tobacco and drinking beer, from his superior, the older tramp.

Discussing the Childs-Drexel home set up for infirm or retired printers, M. Stanislaus Murphy characterized the tramp: "An old gray-haired man, feeble and with tottering footsteps, hobbled into an office recently, looking for work. He appeared weary and footsore, and was evidently broken up. Upon his features were traces of care and anxiety, and a more forlorn and dejected looking being I had not met for a long time."

But on learning there was no work, his appeal for charity immediately touched the hearts of the assembled compositors. For we know

> Printers are generous to a fault — no just appeal for charity ever goes unheeded — if they have not got the money they will borrow and return it not again, perhaps. They abhor hypocrisy — no man can deceive them with "honeyed words," if they are not true the typo knows it instinctively; they are not church goers, as a rule, for too many policy men occupy the pulpits these days, and they cannot abide men who are neither hot nor cold. They are good critics and generally just; they are intelligent, well read, unassuming, polite; some of them may be too fond of woman, judging from the number of divorces; they are law-abiding citizens, honest, public spirited, industrious, and kind to their families: nervous, thin and cadaverous; can enjoy a good joke, a good lecture, a good cigar, and,

if strongly tempted, a good drink. They are the personification of patience and do credit to their patron saint—Job; and through his influence and the sufferings they endure striving to benefit humanity it is commonly believed that not a single typo will be excluded from the "better country," although it is acknowledged that some of the craft will have a very close call and be compelled to give divers and sundry excuses to Saint Peter before they reach a "sit" that has no take.[5]

Here, again, the pious closing is typical of the Victorian era. There were many extended metaphors in the form of sermons or poems about this eternal "sit" in the sky:

All proof must be corrected before the final "lock-up," when the columns of our characters are emptied from the "sticks" of habit upon the galleys of our daily lives, and when these are transferred into the chases of life's lost possibilities it is too late to correct the proof. Death with ponderous mallet drives the "quoins" until the pulse stops beating and the eyes of the worn-out compositor are touched with the death-glaze. All revisions of proof are forever closed.[6]

On the road the tramping printer "Wears OLD Shoes" as the type specimen texts of the *fin-de-siècle* have informed us.[7] And we find this in an "Exchange":

It is a fact that there is no class of men so fond of wearing old shoes as printers. It isn't because they don't dress well, for there is no class of men better dressed than they are. Why is it? It is because the men stand on their feet nearly the whole day, and as it is said old shoes come next to a clear conscience for solid comfort, the printers are trying to get their share of the said comfort. If the older and more dilapidated the shoes, the more comfort, some of the "comps" are evidently getting more than their share of this world's blessings. For such shoes! Ye gods! The veriest tramp—outside the trade—would scorn to wear such shoes, but would go barefooted in mid-winter first. Not so with the printer. The "fast" man, the "rusher," the "pounder," the "catch-lots-of-galleys" man, and the proverbial "slow" man, one and all, wear them, and if the "devil" happens to sweep them up with an eye to working them off in a bag of paper on an unsuspecting ragman, the printer will make more fuss than he would if he had lost his best girl.

The "Exchange" was a way to provide entertaining filler for a publication: a bit like forwarded humorous e-mail, it was brief and imaginative, e.g.:

CERTAINLY

In the absence of the regular golf editor, the following question from a beginner was referred to the turf editor for an answer: "In a game of golf is it right to fuzzle your putt, or is it better to fetter on the tee?" The turf editor set his teeth firmly, stared hard at the nail in front of him a few moments, and wrote the following reply: "In case a player snaggles his iron it is permissible for him to fuzzle his putt, but a better plan would be for him to drop his guppy into the pringle and snoodle it out with a niblick."
— *Chicago Tribune*, January 1898.

E. J. Hobsbawm's enlightening article, "The Tramping Artisan," informs us that tramping arrangements among calico-printers, paper-makers and compositors were so well advanced at the turn of the nineteenth century in Britain, that they must have flourished for quite a while before then.

The man who wished to leave town to look for work elsewhere, re-ceived a "blank" or "clearance" or "document" showing him to be a member in good standing of the society. This he presented to the local secretary or relieving officer in the "lodge house" or "club house" or "house of call" of the strange town—generally a pub—re-ceiving in return supper, lodging, perhaps beer and a tramp allow-ance. If there was work to be found, he took it; the "call-book" (if there was one) was of course kept at the house of call, an unofficial local labour exchange. If there was none he tramped on. Should he not get permanent enough work to transfer to a new union branch, the traveller would in due course return to his home town, having made the round of all the branches: among the compositors this grand tour was about 2800 miles long in the 1850s.[8]

One reason for tramping, says Hobsbawm, was to guarantee work or at least relief during a strike. It would keep the unemployed from places of slack trade and prevent victimization.

But in America there was great westward expansion after the Civil War and a resumed boom in newspapers which meant that skilled artisans could find work in most towns. The Civil War indeed could have been a factor in creating a rootless population (if, like today, there were many veterans among the homeless population). John E. Hicks talks about the Missouri River "Pirates" and their habits:

> Of the early day vintage of Pirates was "Judge" Grigsby. On my way to Sedalia, I ran across him near the little town of Knob Noster. He was dressed in a frock coat, white waistcoat, striped trousers, immaculate linen and patent-leather shoes — all topped by a silk hat. He was one of the most picturesque of the old tourist printers, one who never rode in boxcars, but did his traveling either on the velvet cushions or on foot. I believe he preferred the latter mode as being more cognate with his philosophy of a leisurely and gracious manner of spending one's life. As we walked along, he told me something of his theory of life: To live fully and richly, to acquire the greatest delight for the mind in the joys of intellectual curiosity. He would study, he said, the text of nature and the book of life, learning from things about him. He quoted Rousseau to the effect that the only way to travel was on foot while one reveled in the freshness and harmony beside the little streams. Railroads and steamboats, he said, had robbed the pilgrimages of journeymen workers of their poetry, thereby shortening their journey of life.[9]

Reaching his destination — Saint Louis — Hicks continues:

> The *Globe-Democrat* was the place for traveling printers to show up. McCullagh, perhaps remembering his own days as a typesetter, had devised something for the itinerant who happened to be "down on his luck." This was what were known as the "grasshopper cases." Whenever a tourist printer failed to catch on as a sub he was permitted to tackle the "grasshopper cases," set a couple of thousand ems from reprint copy, cash in at the regular scale — and eat.

In the 1832 autobiography of Thomas Gent of York, the vitriolic and contentious Irishman also wrote about tramping printers, or strollers as he called them, in *Teague's Ramble,* "a satire I had written on some of our profession, who richly deserved for their unmerciful usage to me & others, their fellow-creatures; wherein only the guilty were made to feel its sting, and the innocent commended."

Gent wrote of his employees:

> Another journeyman was John Brooker, originally from Ireland; little better, when mellow, than a lunatic, and, quite drunk, a perfect madman. Another was called Thomas Dickenson, a sort of interloper but a good workman, considering his lameness; saucy, sly, conceited, and very offensive when there was no other occasion, but only requiring him to be cleanly, and not offensive to others by his rubbish, which his unreasonable covetousness would not allow time to make away. He had been long in Scotland, where he married; became a stroller; was sent from constable to constable, to Belfrey's parish; afterwards wrought at Doncaster with Mr. Ward; and, at length, died in or near London. I had also for my journeyman, Mr. Pattison, a goodnatured, honest Scot, the best that ever I knew of that sort; and Smith, of the same country, but I think as false a loon as ever came out of it. I was often grieved that my necessity should oblige me to employ some of those ungrateful vermin, and others, particularly one Jackson, a mean senseless wretch, to whom I yet gave the best London prices.[10]

But the system became strained beyond its capacity. In his 1857 autobiography, *The Working Man's Way in the World,* Charles Manby Smith wrote about tramps who would show up for work, get an advance to secure lodging and disappear.

> Owing to the want of any efficient system of union among the members of the trade, the practice of tramping had, at the time I speak of, risen to a most disgraceful climax. A regular tide of lazy and filthy vagabonds, professedly of various trades, but virtually living without work, or the intention of working, flowed lazily through the kingdom from one end of it to the other. These were a continual

and heavy tax upon the industrious members of the several trades upon whom they levied contributions for their support. Their laziness was comparable only to their impudence; it was impossible to get rid of them without a contribution, and if this fell short of their expectations it was not unfrequently received with contemptuous upbraidings. The greatest misfortune that could befall a regular tramp was the finding of employment; and it was rare, indeed, that any effectual assistance could be obtained from one of the tribe. It was necessary, too, to keep a sharp look-out upon their motions, as one and all seemed to possess an uniform habit of converting into cash, at the pawn-shop, anything and everything furtively portable. Like every other trade, that of the tramp has undergone the pressure of competition; they are as numerous as they ever were, perhaps more so; but necessity has taught them civility, and, finding the mere plea of want of work in most cases ineffectual to raise supplies, they invent wives and children starving, sick families or domestic calamities, and find it still difficult, at least according to the confessions of some of them, to escape the occasional pressure of hunger during their wanderings. There wants but the exercise of a little firmness and common sense on the part of the inmates of our workshops to put an end, at once and for ever, to this wretched trade — a trade by which thousands of indolent scamps contrive to get through life without discharging its duties, submitting to the vilest degradation, and enduring every species of discomfort—for all which they yet find compensation in the darling pleasures of a nomadic wayside existence. A point-blank refusal of money, in every case, would be an act of humanity to the tramps themselves, by putting an end to their miserable wanderings, and would relieve the working-classes from a burdensome tax, which it is injustice, not charity, to submit to.[11]

Finding no work in London, Smith, himself, tramped to Paris where he worked on pirated editions of Byron and Walter Scott for Galignani.

Speaking of "Typographical Tourism" in Britain, the Webbs wrote, "The 'Wanderjahre,' or customary years of travel from town to town at the close of apprenticeship were unknown as a regular custom in this country."[12] There were reasons for strong unions and traditions of seven-year apprenticeships:

> We have here a handicraft requiring no small degree of education and manual dexterity, which has ranked, from the outset, as a highly skilled craft. ... Nor has the trade become any easier to learn. Neither machinery nor division of labor has yet enabled the capitalist employer to split up the old craft into sections, each calling only for a low grade of skill. [*footnote:* The most improved machine, the Linotype, demands, indeed, an even higher level of skill and a more varied proficiency than that of the compositor at case.] Employers and workmen still agree that the only way to attain proficiency is for a boy to be put through a prolonged course of actual technical instruction in a number of separate processes, from deciphering manuscripts to "displaying" advertisements.

And while Craftsmens' Clubs excluded from membership any who had not undergone the rigorous seven-year apprenticeship there were other ways of acquiring the skill:

> The Trade Union does not even hear of the numerous instances in which a printing press is set up in the basement of a great advertising manufacturer who chooses to do his own printing on the premises. In all such cases the employment of boy-labor is absolutely unrestricted in numbers, and unregulated by any educational requirements. The standard of quality and speed of working is of the lowest, but the youth who in such shops picks up an elementary acquaintance with "case," presently gets taken on as a cheap "improver" by the little country stationer, and eventually, whether competent or not, drifts to London to pick up casual employment as a journeyman.[13]

Major tramping groups in Britain were masons, compositors and ironfounders: in the 1840s as many as 25% of compositors were on the road. "Between 1880 and 1889 tramp relief amounted to between 20-40% of unemployed relief; between 1890 and 1899 between 6 and 20%; between 1900 and 1906 it was never more than 8% and fell as low as 5%. The tramping printer was rapidly becoming extinct."[14] Hobsbawm thinks the tram played a role: it did not even mean a decline in long-distance mobility. Furthermore Unions became better organized and also offered emigration benefits, although these never caught on. Hobsbawm doesn't mention it, but obviously the Linotype[15] was partly responsible (despite the comps' ridicule that only a machine that could think could possibly replace them).

> These [composing and distributing] machines began to be used about 1876, but owing to the imperfections of the earlier inventions, it was not until the last decade of the century that their competition with the old hand compositor came to be seriously felt. The advent of the machine has throughout been most distasteful to the men. But the Compositors' Trade Unions have from the first disclaimed any desire to prevent its introduction, or to forbid the members to work it. Their policy has been to secure the new employment to their own members on terms which protected their Standard Rate.[16]

In the eighteenth century compositors were paid by the job and even after hourly wages were established some shops kept the old system. Typically newspaper compositors were paid by the galley, which took about four hours to fill. But occasionally the compositors were asked to "pull out," that is speed up and set more than a quarter of a galley in an hour to meet a deadline. This of course garnered a bonus.[17]

One non-Union printer who left a rich account of his experiences in small shops in Britain was William Adams who ended his long career as a reformer and newspaperman with an autobiography, *Memoirs of a Social Atom* (1903). He fancied the life of a tramp and tried it for a few years, though he left the dives full of fidgety and snoring drunks with a few fleas. In an anecdote he introduces us to the printer's pie (known in the US by its Greek cognomen of "pi"):

> There is a story of a Leicester journalist who, when an accident had occurred on the eve of publication, went to press with a column of pie, preceded by this intimation — "Our Dutch mail has just arrived. Having no time to translate the despatch, we give it in the original."

The Manchester Typographical Society was riven by a major crisis when it tried to abolish tramping in 1851; also, noted from the 1849 minutes: "You know what the condition of the tramp is. The man's appearance is a discredit to the profession he has spent seven years in acquiring the art of. ... As a class those who tramp are little short of lost creatures."

A speaker at the 1856 delegate meeting said, "he knew men who had been on the road ever since he was an apprentice. It was impossible to end tramping because of the vast number of incorrigible characters in the profession."

But the demon drink can certainly be said to play a role in the wanderlust, as reported in the *Scottish Typographical Circular*, March 1859:

> "I always observed," wrote an old compositor in 1859, "That those trades who had settled wages, such as masons, wrights, painters, etc., and who were obliged to attend regularly at stated hours, were not so much addicted to day drinking as printers, bookbinders, tailors, shoemakers, and those tradesmen who generally were on piecework, and not so much restricted in regard to their attendance at work except when it was particularly wanted."[18]

By the end of the century tramping was accepted, especially in America with its vast spaces between cities. *The Pacific Union Printer* (August 1893) ran a bunch of in-jokes about tramps under the heading "SOCIETY NOTES":

> The Brake-Beam Route is the most popular with tourists nowadays.
>
> *
>
> Sir William Tule, the millionaire, is in the interior studying horticulture.
>
> *
>
> The secretary has discarded optical mourning and is now a shining light in the Club Fistiana.
>
> *

Manager Getthere of our baseball club, which met on the field of battle with the Sacramento club Sunday, denies the allegation that a part of the uniform of his aggregation consisted of corsets.

*

The fear is expressed that unless the frigidity of the atmosphere on the Rue de Clay is not lessened soon, W. McAllister Smithian will have to seek conservatories anew to secure his usual boutonaires.

*

Arrivals at the Hotel del Conboy are said to have been numerous of late. Jose Bartholomew, however, recently declined to accept a hospitable invitation to sojourn there, but his traveling companion decided to remain till fall.

*

Colonel Sellers is in doubt, in order to go on his usual summer vacation, whether to accept the twenty-dollar union donation or lasso the rudder of an outgoing deep-water vessel and then tying the other end of the riata around his body.

* * *

From the notorious to the obscure, many who labored at the press left us written impressions. David R. Locke assumed the persona of the Rev. Petroleum Vesuvius Nasby, of the Church of the Slawtered Innocents, becoming an instant best-seller (and Lincoln's favorite author) with his political satires written from Confedrit X Roads in Kentucky. Twain recalled:

> [Locke] left school at an early age and was apprenticed to a printer, after which he worked on a succession of newspapers. At the out-break of the Civil War he was the owner and editor of the Bucyrus (Ohio) *Journal*. It was not until a year later that he published his first satirical piece as Petroleum V. Nasby, an ignorant, bigoted, and boorish character who promoted liberal causes by seeming to oppose them.[19]

Journalist Henry W. Shaw, under the pen name "Josh Billings," wrote lots of one-liners, also in folksy dialect, impossible to slog through today; while Charles Bertrand Lewis's *nom-de-plume* ("M. Quad") betrays his craft background. Also known as the *Detroit Free Press* man, his story, "Old Frisket," tells of some jours who get the small town editor drunk and put out a paper full of outrageous statements about the townspeople. R. A. Thomas' "Morningstar," included here, has the same prank.

Mark Twain says he learned how to write from Bret Harte, another compositor, whom he met in San Francisco. Both men borrowed from the great humorist "Artemus Ward" (Charles F. Browne [1834–67]) who started out at the typestand in Maine, in Boston, and various papers in Ohio.

Hicks puts Twain's fame in perspective:

> Some of the older persons in Hannibal remembered him as a "start-natured fool" who used to "fool around the print shop." He had written a book or two, they understood, which they hadn't read, but which the newspapers said were good. Still, they couldn't believe Sam Clemens would amount to much. He was too fond of playing jokes.[20]

Another famous American printer was Horace Greeley, "The 'Tramp' Printer who became a Power in Politics, a Maker of History, and America's Foremost Journalist," according to an article in *The New York Times* on the centenary of his birth in 1911: "Like Jackson and Grant, Greeley was of Scotch descent, enriched and softened with a blend of Irish. And like these famous men, he was, if not a typical American, of a type that America alone has produced." Out of his apprenticeship, young Horace tramped to New York, and because he was a gawky bumpkin, a printer decided to play a trick on him and gave him a job setting a New Testament in Pearl type, on a narrow measure with copious italic, Greek and superscript. The lad succeeded and from that day on did not lack for employment.[21]

In his first collection of stories, *Vissch*, Will L. Visscher recalls "A Whole Lot of Them," including

WALLACE GRUELLE

Was a born poet, worked on more newspapers than it would be possible to enumerate; always cared more for the dress of nature than his own; has been a soldier, a Good Templar and a good fellow, and is now editing a country paper in Kentucky.

HOWARD R. HETRICK

Is a regular Bohemian. He would just as soon start for a trip to the Kamschatkians without a nickle, as to go with his pockets full of the filthy lucre, and he would get through all the same. With the exception of about a year and a half, roaming between Easton, Pennsylvania, and Brownsville, Texas, and San Francisco, California, "Het" has been the city editor of the *St. Joseph Herald*. He knows everybody in the city and, moreover, has a "nose" for news, and as a reporter he is unexcelled.

CHARLIE MORSE

Noted as being a first-class news-editor, went West; was killed by the Indians through the newspapers, but turned up afterward, "as well and as hearty as he ever was," with more hair than usual, and now manipulates a Buffalo paper, which perhaps he became acquainted with on the plains.

A. D. SIMMONS

Seldom says anything unless it is necessary. He is the commercial editor of the *Kansas City Times*, and a good one. Simmons has been the rounds, and is a first-class Western newspaper man in any capacity. He has, like other Bohemians, had a mixed time of it, having worked on many different papers in as many different cities. He is small, lithe, active and unassuming, and goes along about his business just like a man who knows exactly what he wants, and he generally gets it.

GEORGE PERKINS

Is by all odds the best-dressed man in Kansas City, and is a remarkably able editor for one of his age. He first broke out in Fort Scott as a Faber consumer, then became city editor of the *News* in

Kansas City, then associate editor of the Cincinnati *Chronicle*, then chief editor of the *Kansas City Bulletin*. He has traveled among the scenes of Burns' and Scott's poems, and is altogether a warm-hearted gentleman, who will shine from high places before his sun goes down.

JESSIE WHITEHEAD

This gentleman is quiet, unassuming and clever. He writes beautiful poetry and does well anything else that is required of him in the newspaper line, except to drink intoxicating beverages and live on nothing. As a traveling correspondent he is an unequivocal success. But he has quit that, and is a general utility man on the editorial work of the *Kansas City Bulletin*.

I have included two stories of women compositors although, in general, women were not found among the tramps (unless a printer persuaded one to elope with him). Women compositors (referred to patronizingly as "Setting Hens" or vulgarly as "Two-Nicks") earned lower wages and could be used as strike-breakers. However in 1869 the Typographical Union admitted women as members, stipulating that they get the same wages as men. One of our two stories comes, via an "Exchange," from the Denver press and was picked up by the *Carrier Dove* in Oakland. This paper was a Spiritualist weekly, edited by Mrs. Julia S. F. Schlesinger, who transformed it into a voice for female suffrage.[22] It was printed by the Women's Co-operative Printing Union, an all-female shop that flourished in San Francisco between the Gold Rush of 1849 and the '06 Quake.

1. Thomas MacKellar, The Doom of the Printer, in *Tam's Fortnight Ramble*, Philadelphia, 1847.

2. Quoted in Patrick Duffy, *The Skilled Compositor*, Aldershot, 2000, p. 102.

3. J. B. Graham, *Handset Reminiscences*, Salt Lake City, 1915, p. 72.

4. *The American Model Printer*, vol. 1, no. 1, New York, October 1879, p. 7.

5. William M. Cubery, *Fifty Years a Printer*, San Francisco, 1900, pp. 11-2.

6. "We Are All Type-Setters," from *Lectures Containing the Best Thoughts from the Lectures, Sermons, and Writings of William E. Hall*, Philadelphia: the Author, c. 1886. This sermon was found as an "Exchange" in the English typographic trade journal *Hailing's Circular* (Spring, 1886).

7. Palmer & Rey specimen book, 1892, p. 220. See my *Alphabets to Order* (London, 2000) for a discussion of the Tramping texts in type specimens of the period.

8. "Typographical Reminiscences" by an old Typo, *Typographical Circular*, June 1891, p. 8, quoted by E. J. Hobsbawm, "The Tramping Artisan" in *The Economic History Review*, Second Series, vol. III, no. 3, 1951, p. 299.

9. John Edward Hicks, *Adventures of a Tramp Printer*, Kansas City, 1950, p. 36.

10. Thomas Gent, *The Life of Mr Thomas Gent, Printer of York*, London, 1832, p. 174.

11. Charles Manby Smith, *The Working Man's Way in the World*, London: W. & F. G. Cash, 1857. But see Rounsfell, *On the Road* (Horsham, 1982), for the story of a tramp who knew how to work the system to advantage without being a bum.

12. Sidney and Beatrice Webb, *Industrial Democracy*, London, 1897; reprinted 1920, 1965, p. 455, note 1. There were also Antipodean tramps: see "A Veteran Tramp," *American Model Printer*, vol. 1, no. 5, pp. 66-7.

13. Webb, p. 465.

14. Hobsbawm, p. 311.

15. "In 1893 the Linotype came over the typographical horizon, sending most of the old Birds scurrying to some other business." John Gordon, *A Memorial to the Tramp Printer*, South Brewer, Maine, 1927, p. 15.

16. Webb, pp. 406-7.

17. See Webb, p. 436, note 2; see also p. 287, and pp. 298-9 on piecework vs hourly wages and the division of "Fat" (sometimes known as "Phat").

18. Quoted in Webb pp. 326-7, footnote.

19. Smith, *Autobiography of Mark Twain*, Berkeley, UC Press, 2010, p. 506.

20. Hicks, p. 49.

21. Horace Greeley, *Recollections of a Busy Life*, New York, 1868, pp. 85-6.

22. Roger Levenson, *Women in Printing, Northern California 1857-90*, Santa Barbara, 1994, pp. 159-60.

Passing of The Tourist.

AT A BANQUET in Kansas City a few nights ago William Allen White, the editor of the Emporia *Gazette*, responded to the toast "The tramp printer," and among other things, said:

"In the morning he used to sit humped over the primer case throwing in a handful. When the editor came to work, it was customary for the others in the shop to show the editor some attention; the foreman to walk to the editorial desk with the proof of an ad; the job printer to hammer busily with a planer on the form of a 'rooms to rent' card, which was ever being made ready for the press; the two lean compositors to shake their cases as though they had been working for hours; the cub to change legs on the job press and clatter the throw off with more business than a bird pup. But the tourist — the typographical tourist — at the primer case, paid no homage to rank: made no unmanly obsequious demonstration before potentates and powers. He kept on, rattling the types in their boxes, as though nothing unusual had happened. After a whispered dialogue between the foreman and the editor, explaining the stranger's presence, it was the editorial privilege to approach the throne. If it was winter the editor might saunter out to the stove, and back up to it with palms outstretched.

"Then he was permitted by the tourist to ask: 'Where you from?' After receiving a reply the editor was expected to ask 'Well, how's work there?' To this the answer required by an unwritten yet inviolable law of the craft was 'damn rotten!'

"Thereafter the editor might resume his work or inquire about old friends, or take up the regular order, or proceed to unfinished business. For the tramp printer had been duly and formally installed and the opening services were closed. To the layman all this pomp & circumstance of welcoming the tourist may seem empty and idle. Yet the arrival of the tramp printer at the country office twenty years ago meant to the craftsmen there what the return of Lentulus with victorious legions meant to Capus; what the delegation from the grand lodge, ready to give out the new password and exemplify the work, means to the brethren: what the visit of an ordaining bishop to convey the apostolic succession means to churchmen, and what the coming of a new star means to an astrologer.

"For the tramp printer brought the light into dark places. If there was a new ink reducer in vogue, the tourist knew it and could make it. He showed the foreman how to set the disc of the jobber and print in colors. The tramp could make paste that would never sour and tabletting glue that would stick and never crack nor melt in all eternity. He could whittle out a line of wood letter or make slugs. He could tie a string to an end of the folding table and cut two folios from a quarto as fast as the devil could fold. He could make rollers that would print a hair line of script, or bring out the dapple in the flanks of the iron gray stallion for the livery stable job. He could cut out reprint with his rule for the copy hook when the old man was away, and he could go to the nonpareil case and set up a piece of poetry for the first column from memory. He was guide, philosopher and friend to the editor, and to the back room he revived the world, the flesh and devil. Peter B. Lee, 'Old Slugs' and Biggsby — whither have they gone? — those old style faces with the hair lines all over them, with their condensed Gothic noses, with their wrong font eyes, with their mouths blacksmithed full of fine cut to justify with their double pica cheeks! Poor old typographical errors; they were cast before the days of the point system and they have been thrown into the hell box of oblivion.

"Yet they did their work well. They fullfilled their mission in the world. The tramp printer's labor-saving devices, perfected and carried to their ultimate conclusions, have become great inventions of this printing craft. Archimedes said if he had a proper lever he would move the world. The lazy tramp printer who first rolled a cylinder over a form of types found the Archimedean lever. That lever has moved the world further in a century than it had moved before in a thousand years. Its unknown inventor was as surely inspired, was as surely working a divine purpose toward man as was he who chiseled the law upon the stone at Sinai. For that printer's lever has twisted away the scepters of kings and has put royal power into the hands of the people. That lever has pried the world from ignorant selfishness to intelligent human brotherhood. That lever has lifted man so high that the Golden Rule has ceased to be merely a theological precept, but has become the heart of civilization, the soul of the legal code, the ideal of its commercial ethics."

THE
GREAT
AMERICAN

PETER
BARTLETT

TYPO-
GRAPHICAL
TOURIST

PETER BARTLETT LEE, the great American pedestrian and typographical tourist, arrived in this city at 4 a.m. yesterday. He is a philosopher who has devoted his life to studying the changes of government, and their effects upon the people. In order to do this thoroughly and effectually, it keeps him constantly traveling. His last trip was over the "hog-back" of Missouri, as he scientifically describes the Ozark Hills. He states that the 25 years' experience he has had in going to and fro upon the earth leads him to conclude that the world is growing worse. "Take," says Peter, "the true standard of human happiness and the basis of prosperity — the price of whisky. In the days of *ante bellum* it was three cents a drink and trust; now it is fifteen cents and 'no trust' staring you in the face from the walls of every hostelrie."

"No," said P. B. Lee, mournfully, "times ain't what they used to be," and, dropping the 3-em space with which he had been unconsciously toying, he said: "Gimme four-bits!"

Peter Bartlett Lee has a pass over every railroad in the United States; but he says he can't utilize them, for "it always makes his feet sore to ride in the cars." There is not a railroad bridge in the United States but bears the impress of his fingers and toe nails, as he "cooned" across; nor is there the hum of a telegraph wire in the United States but what he recognizes.

His experience would fill a volume of strange adventure. Many an inclement night some simple farmer, living remote from lines of trade and travel, has heard a knock at his door, and, upon opening it, was greeted with the apparition of a gaunt and seedy stranger, balanced on each side with a mutton-chop whisker, and whose body swayed to one side as a counterpoise to a roll of newspaper exchanges, which he carried under the opposite arm.

This would be Peter B. Lee, who wanted a night's lodging.

Permission to enter being granted, Peter would soon be comfortably seated beside the blazing hearth, and his social powers would soon disarm all suspicion. The exchanges would be unfolded, and ere an hour the entire household would be intently interested in the doings in the great world around them, as eloquently read by Peter Bartlett. The delight which he at first inspired by his pleasing powers of description ascended into awe at the deep and profound knowledge he displayed on subjects of political economy, while from the rich library of his memory he would unfold volume after volume of historical lore.

In two hours, Peter Bartlett would be a general favorite and a welcome member of a happy household; in two more, he would be snugly asleep in the best bed in the best room in the house. Two or three days will P. B. thus rest and recruit his tired body, when he will again to the road, taking the earnest wishes of that household, who watch from the portal the retreating figure of this strange and mysterious visitor as he fades into the dim shadows that form the barriers between them and the great world without. But though he may never again appear to them, that family will never forget the visit of Peter Bartlett Lee.

Equally at home is Peter Bartlett in the large city, and his first visit is generally to that temple of information and useful knowledge — the printing office.

No matter what part of the union it may be in, the moment he arrives a general yell of recognition goes up as he enters the composing room, and a volley of inquiries and exclamations rattle around the alleys:

"Hello, Pete! how's the walking?"

"Pete, did you come in on a Pullman?"

"Peter Bartlett, ain't you so tired of sitting down, yer feet ache!"

"O, shoot the nose!"

"Hevings! what a hat!" and a thousand other expressions and ironical suggestions greet him on all sides.

Peter Bartlett gravely bows until the confusion subsides, when he advances and receives a hearty greeting from the typo throng assembled. The next thing Peter B. does, however, is to proceed to business, and the whole office is laid under contribution, which is duly presented to him as "a testimonial of respect."

Peter immediately disappears, and in 20 minutes has persuaded the nearest saloon-keeper that he is the new railroad superintendent just appointed.

When this first installment of lucre is gone, he tackles the editorial room, and rarely fails to make a raise. And when this and all other sources of financial replenishment are exhausted, Peter Bartlett gets another bundle of exchanges and again starts out on his endless journey — a Typographical Wandering Jew!

There are worse men than he who are wanderers, and when his last tramp is ended at the edge of that "Dark River," may Charon be kind and Pluto gracious, as they ferry across the disembodied spirit of Peter Bartlett Lee.

The Old-time Printer.

NOW THAT A PRINTER AND PUBLISHER has been elected president of the United States, and another printer and publisher was an aspirant for the same honor, the country has naturally been awakened to a keener interest in the "art preservative," and has focused attention on a craft which has provided big men for every position in life. That two men of the same vocation should at the same time be the political center of the whole country, emphasises the fact that the school of printers to which they belong is not so nourishing as it was.

Where is the old-fashioned printer? With his disappearance, the world loses a type of worker who, from Ben Franklin on, has furnished the country with men who have made their influence felt, not only as master printers and master journalists, but who, through the liberal education and ideals acquired in their training, have swelled the ranks of the learned professions and become actors, ministers, authors, humorists, and leaders in various lines.

The term "tramp printer" has become of deep reproach, and justly so. The low grade "tramp printer" has always existed since printing began. Nobody disdains him more than the legitimate followers of Caxton, et al., and there will be no lament when the last tramp printer is heard of no more.

But there is a tendency to designate as "tramp printers" a large body of men who do not deserve to be and are wrongly so designated. In former days all printers were recruited from three distinct classes of apprentices. The lines of cleavage between the three were very straightly drawn.

The first and most important class was composed of the elect; the well-born and well-bred; the ambitious young man who desired a higher education and who entered a printing office with the intention of learning the business thoroughly, and fitting himself for a position of importance. The printing office was the poor man's university, and highly esteemed as such.

A few generations ago a college or technical training was not easy to acquire. Youths who today go to colleges and advanced institutions of learning are the class who formerly became apprentices in printing and newspaper offices, and it was perfectly natural, as well as indicative of good judgment and ambition, for the youth with little money and no means of getting any, to climb to his house of dreams thru the medium of the art of printing. By so doing he not only acquired a liberal education and a broad cultural foundation, but he learned a most honorable trade (practically a profession), at which he was always sure of a good livelihood, but he sharpened his wits and acquired initiative and an amazing knowledge of human nature. A newspaper office was the natural forum and gathering place for all the brightest thinkers and of men in the public eye.

To a now almost extinct class of American printers belonged such shining lights as Bayard Taylor, Bret Harte, Artemus Ward, William Dean Howells, Ben Shillabar, Opie Read, Charles B. Lewis, and a whole galaxy of good men and good printers. That the system of becoming printers and writers "through the fingers" was a splendid one, the mere recital of these few names among many, is evidence.

It was natural for men of this stamp to seek to enlarge their knowledge by traveling about the country while they worked at their chosen calling, studying types, gathering local color, and satisfying their desire "strange places to see." Traveling in those days was not as easy and universal as now. Printers traveled afoot when there was anything to see, hear or learn thereby. They patronized the railroads when that best served their turn. They were respected and respectable, they paid their way, and if they were not wealthy why nobody else was, either. When they had absorbed the atmosphere or sights of one place they took the next in which they were interested. They were in no sense "tramp printers," as most people understand the term. When the traveling printer of this first class found his niche, he settled down, and filled it.

It was in this manner that Bayard Taylor, famous author, traveler and diplomat, covered the United States and Europe. A more polished gentleman and a more graceful writer and poet it would be hard to find in his day, and that his "Views Afoot" were acquired while continuing work as a printer, added rather than detracted from their value.

Most of the old-time printers were writers as well. They gravitated naturally into the writing profession. Not infrequently, too, these newspaper men and the humorists who conducted or contributed columns of humor, set much of their matter "right outer their heads" at the case. It seemed at one time as though every good American humorist had been a traveling printer at one time or another.

Ben Shillabar's Mrs. Partington and Ike made their debut in the columns of the Boston *Post*. Artemus Ward hiked all the way from Portland, Maine, to Boston and then by easy stages to Cleveland, Ohio. En route he studied human nature, gathered local color, making the acquaintance of theatrical and circus people of every type, gradually visualizing in his own imagination that showman through whose mouth he later launched himself into fame. The idea which he acquired as a traveling printer came to fruition while he was on the *Plain Dealer* of Cleveland.

Some of Ward's biographers endeavor to show that the gentle and witty Artemus was a "tramp printer" — dissipated and an irresponsible ne'er-do-well. He has been greatly maligned, for he was a man of keen insight and a real Yankee for shrewdness. Charles B. Lewis, known and beloved by millions as "M. Quad," the creator of Mr. Bowser, was a traveling printer of the school which is no more.

"Texas Jack" was another aristocrat of printerdom who elected to travel. After walking from Springfield he entered into a Worcester, Massachusetts, daily composing room and asked to "sub." He was tall and gawky, wore a sombrero, top boots and a long linen duster. He was set to work, but his countrified appearance and retiring manner promptly started the compositors to guying him, "Who is Slug Three?" "Who's the Dutchman that sets this take?" "What blacksmith shop was Slug Three raised in?" and similar cutting remarks for Texas Jack's edification were freely bandied about.

The Southerner, however, paid no attention to these thrusts. He kept right on sticking type. By and by it became evident that the stranger was far from being the countryman he looked, for he "emptied in" with amazing frequency, and his proof showed no errors.

In the morning it developed that "Texas Jack" had outstripped the old guard. He had set a string* of 11,000 ems, a record never touched, for the time consumed, except by the exceptional "swift." Pocketing his big earnings, the traveling printer gave a farewell salute to the jeerers of the night before. "Good day, gentlemen," he said politely, with a courtly bow, and a graceful wave of the sombrero, as he smilingly withdrew.

The second class of printers were those who took up printing because it was a good trade and regarded as on a higher plane than some others. Most of the members of this class had aspirations common to all respectable craftsmen: they hoped to own their own shops in time, and they planned and saved to

---

* String is used to measure the amount of matter set by the comp each shift.

that end. They were honest and reliable workmen, and a few of this type still turn to printing today, but their number, too, is constantly diminishing. The printing business, as a rule, is not conducive to getting rich quick, and more attractive and hotter paying opportunities in other trades, as well as changes in the trade itself, have much decreased the number of this class of recruits. Farsighted employing printers are recognizing the seriousness of the shortage of good material for printers, and are endeavoring to make the business more attractive to those choosing a trade.

Typical of this class of printers was "Shortalize" Murray. Murray may have been named after the grammarian, but he was merely "Shortalize" to us because he always spoke of "shortalizing" words. The first day he favored the offices with his services he broke the silence by looking up from his case and solemnly inquiring: "How do you shortalize 'secretary' here?" He was told the office style of abbreviating, but the nickname "Shortalize" was his from that day forth.

"Shortalize" had worked in nearly every large printing office, except some in the largest cities, in the United States and Canada. He was thrifty. When he reached our office he usually liked to stay for some time partly because the editor had a dog which helped "Shortalize" defeat the high cost of living. It was in the lean '70s, when prices after the war were so high they almost touched the sky — or present-day records. "Shortalize" used to board himself. When he did his marketing, old Rover, the editor's dog, used to accompany him. "Shortalize," pointing to the animal, would ask for "five cents' worth of meat for the dog."

Rover was a large Newfoundland, with a peculiarly hungry expression. The dealer, after a glance at the animal, and knowing that his owner was a lone bachelor and boarded at the sorry village "hotel," was usually very generous. In those days a nickel would buy enough to last several meals, so "Shortalize" would live high on next to nothing.

Alexander Cameron, a Scotsman, was a most lovable, most irritating, and a most amusing specimen of this type of traveling knight-errant. Aleck had been working in a certain office for some time, when he incurred the wrath of his employer because of a breach of discipline.

Alexander came to work just as if he had not received his discharge.

"No use, Aleck," said his exasperated boss. "You're discharged. You can't stay another minute."

Alexander Cameron calmly continued removing his coat and rolling up his shirt sleeves.

"Did you hear what I said, Aleck?" demanded his wrathy superior. "You may go. You're discharged."

"Why, Mr. Lenox," returned Aleck in a shocked tone, "Do ye think I'll be mean enough to leave ye now, with all this work? No, no, Mr Lenox. Ye little know Alexander Cameron if ye think that. I'll never desert ye, Mr. Lenox, never! Just count on Aleck every time." He stayed.

The third and lowest class of printers comprised those who simply drifted into the business, or who failed to make good at the trade. From this class came the genuine tramp printer. He is still with us. The quality, never very good, has steadily deteriorated and the modern tramp printer is more "tramp" and less printer than ever before. The general public too often has formed its opinions of printers in general from this sorry class. The old-time tramp printer was generally "an amoosing cuss," as Artemus Ward would say.

STUART CAMERON

STUART CAMERON was a regular contributor to *The Printer and Bookmaker*, writing on such topics as "Printers as 'Popular Authors,'" a favourite subject among journeymen. Starting with the contributions to classical scholarship of the Manutii and Estiennes he gives a roll-call of famous printers who turned author, like Samuel Richardson, "a goody-goody, even somewhat dull English printer," who "produced works which made him pre-eminently the popular author of his day, at a time, too, when the real genius of Henry Fielding, with all his superior advantages of university training, was contending for the prize of popularity in the same field." Cameron's highest praise is reserved for Rétif de la Bretonne, the voluminous French author who wrote his works in the typestick, "thus pursuing the work of composition in a double sense." Other Frenchmen, including the revolutionary philosopher Pierre Proudhon, Pierre-Jean Béranger, and mystic Socialist Pierre Leroux also labored at the type-stand. In England and Ireland, Cameron finds Douglas Jerrold, the now-forgotten novelists Benjamin Farjeon (who prospected and printed in Australia & New Zealand), Captain Mayne Reid and John Boyle O'Reilly.

Surveying the field of contemporary printer-authors in North America, Cameron notes:

Mr. Clemens, who, as Mark Twain, has had one of the most successful careers in the history of popular authorship, worked at the case in his time, and is still remembered by certain veteran Western printers as a good fellow, even if, as one of them once said, he was "slower than the wrath of God." The connection of Bret Harte and Mr. Howells with the craft is well known, and both of these gentlemen are popular authors in the best sense of the term. Probably two of the most popular lyrics ever produced in this country were "The Old Oaken Bucket" of Woodworth, and Morris' "Woodman, Spare that Tree," and both writers were compositors. Walt Whitman, too, had undergone all the vicissitudes of a printer's life, and while the author of "Leaves of Grass" will probably never be a popular writer, his memory bids fair to outlast generations of smooth versifiers and fastidious critics.

Cameron praises Sylvanus Cobb, Junior, author of the "Gunmaker of Moscow," which he tells us was an early favorite work of fiction. He also mentions the late Colonel E. Z. C. Judson, a larger-than-life rogue who wrote bombastic dime novels under the *nom de plume* Ned Buntline:

Whether Colonel Judson was ever really a printer or not I don't know. He told me that he was one on the only occasion on which I had the honor to see him. The colonel had introduced himself to a party of us in a well-known hostelry on Chatham street. He proved a very welcome addition, and when he assured us that he too had been a compositor we were all prepared to swear that if he was not one he deserved to be. If a vivid imagination alone be sufficient to constitute a popular author a man of genius, my recollections of that evening would lead me to class "Ned Buntline" among the great authors of our country. But it is this very wealth of imagination which led me to withhold implicit credence from his assertion of craft brotherhood, and to suspect that that claim had as little basis as one made by him somewhat later in the evening to have been a mess-mate and favorite officer of the buccaneer Lafitte of Barataria. Still he may have been a compositor — he deserved to be so, as I have said — and not even G. W. M. Reynolds was ever more emphatically a popular author.

from a Rolling Moss Stone

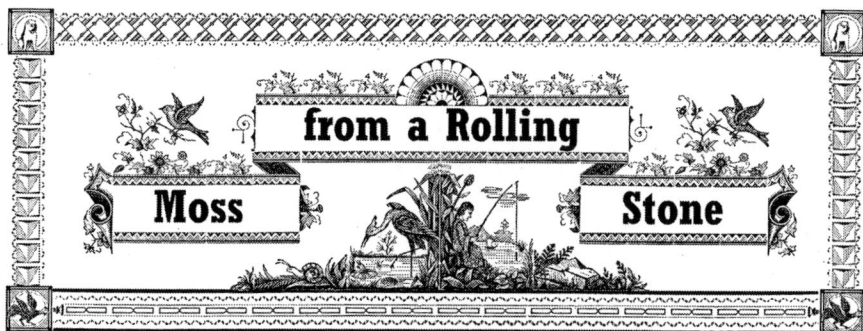

THERE WAS STARTED by a group of enthusiastic Prohibitionists in Buffalo some years ago a paper called the *Sixteenth Amendment* for the purpose of advocating the insertion of an amendment in the Constitution prohibiting the sale of intoxicating liquors. A printer well known in the craft in those days as "Rocky Mountain" Jones interviewed the manager of the new journal regarding the plans and prospects of his venture. The evangelist of prohibition gave an eloquent exposition of the ideas and hopes of those interested in the enterprise, and among other details mentioned that no one would be employed on the paper in any capacity who either drank, swore, or used tobacco in any form. "Well," said "Rocky," as he bade the gentleman good-bye, "I wish you luck, sir, but I'll give you a pointer on one thing — you'll have to import your compositors from the kingdom of heaven."

In this somewhat epigrammatic remark Mr. Jones only gave expression to a very common but not altogether true view of the character of the disciples of Gutenberg. While experience would seem to show that the atmosphere of the composing room is not the most favorable to what some cynics have called the "kindergarten morality," yet many examples could be shown of printers who have possessed all the negative virtues which were demanded from the candidate for employment on the *Sixteenth Amendment*. It must be confessed, however, that the opposite character has been the one most generally found in the craft, and the roystering, happy-go-lucky wanderer has come to be regarded on the whole as the typical compositor.

A friend of mine once told me that when he first entered the country printing office where he learned his trade, the foreman — a gruff, piratical-looking fellow — put him through a sort of catechism.

"Well, boy, you want to be a printer, do you? Do you drink?"

"Oh, no, sir!"

"Do you chew tobacco?"

"No, sir."

"Do you swear?"

"No, indeed, sir."

"Go home — you'll never make a printer."

That is an instance of one of the causes that operate — or did operate in former days, at least — in changing the modest, mild-mannered neophyte into the knowing, would-be "fast" youth of a year or so later, and too often into the finished profligate with whom we are all too familiar. What I mean is, that even the steadiest-going of typesetters seem to take a pride in the evil reputation borne by the craft. I suppose it is the same instinct of our fallen nature to which Balzac has reference when he says that "the most domestic bourgeois is not displeased to hear it hinted that he is a little bit of a roué."

Then the stories the bright, growing lad hears from day to day from his seniors who have been out in that wide, wide world which ever more vividly excites his imagination. It is these tales carelessly told by the transient employee which make the eager, listening boy firmly determine that he, too, will "see the world." And as soon as he has completed his apprenticeship — often, indeed, before — he "takes to the road" and adds one more to the army of "typographical tourists." All this, of course, applies to the state of things as it existed some years ago, before the advent of the machine. Already there are many signs of a great change in this respect, and in so far as the introduction of these machines shall contribute to check the roving spirit among printers it will be an unmixed good.

When I first entered a printing office, the promised land of the Northern compositor was the South. According to the stories told by those who came back from that enchanted land, everything there was different and better than the common, everyday experience of our cold Northern clime could afford. Wages were higher, life was freer — for a white man, of course — men were more generous and braver, women both fairer and kinder. Occasionally the state of society resulting from the "peculiar institution" gave rise to some piece of romance such as could never have happened north of Mason and Dixon's line.

I remember one such story had quite a fascination for me in those days "before the war." The hero of this romance — a rather poor hero, I thought then, and think now — was one Aleck R—, who worked for a short time just previous to the outbreak of the Rebellion in the office where I was serving my time. R. was quite a handsome fellow, with a style of good looks much in vogue in those days — tall, slim, dark, with black curls, he might have just stepped out from the pages of a novelette by Sylvanus Cobb, Jr., or Ned Buntline. Some years before I knew him, R., while working in Cincinnati, formed in some way the acquaintance of a very pretty girl from Tennessee, who was attending a boarding school in that city. She was pretty, the daughter of a Southern planter; it was probable she would be an heiress, and the mercenary Adonis put more vim in his love-making than he had ever before thought it worth while to do. The consequence was that, what with his good looks and his impassioned speeches, he soon persuaded his fair one to an elopement. They were married hurriedly in Cincinnati, and after a few days proceeded to Tennessee to seek the forgiveness and blessing of the father of the runaway bride. This gentleman, who was a widower, with no other children than this daughter, received the lovers kindly and freely accorded his forgiveness for the precipitate nature of the courtship and marriage which had been transacted without his knowledge. He had a private interview with his son-in-law, however, which somewhat modified the ecstasies of that individual. The planter informed Mr. R. that, while the young lady whom he had married was his only child, she was, unfortunately, the daughter of a quadroon mother. Of course, at that time such a marriage was illegal, but the Southerner proposed that if R. would abide by the consequences of his own act, accept the girl as his wife and take her to Canada to live, he would give him $25,000 down, and as much more at his own death. R. was in love in his way, and he wanted money mighty bad, but the pride of the ante-bellum Caucasian was too strong in him to accept this very fair offer. He abandoned the poor girl, and came back North, to earn his precarious living as a "sub."

Such stories as these made a great impression on the "cubs" of that day, and to travel through the South was the cherished dream of most of the budding printers in the Northern States. Some, many of them, did so shortly afterward in a way that no one dreamed of at the time I speak of, and as a general thing these tourists, with knapsack and rifle, were less favorably impressed either with country or people than were their predecessors of the stick and rule. What between patriotism and the spirit of adventure, the call to arms found a ready response in the ranks of the printing fraternity, who were represented on both sides in the course of "the great misunderstanding."

The war made some men "tramps," probably, who, but for the taste for adventure acquired on the tented field, might never have been tempted to leave their native places. But in the case of the "tramp" printer the disposition to wander is the result of the tradition established by many generations of his predecessors, and sometimes it needs but a seemingly very inadequate cause to set very sedate, matter-of-fact "typos" on their travels.

One I knew who assured me that he had never traveled and had never had the least inclination to do so until, in an evil hour, the malignity of the types had "driven him to the road." He was working in the city where he learned his trade, and one day the editor of the paper on which he was employed had referred in the course of an article to the "soliloquy of Hamlet." The copy was cut into short "takes," and the words "of Hamlet" being in the "take" following my friend's, he did not catch the meaning of the phrase. The article was "rushed" into the paper without reading, and the infuriated writer was made to speak of the "solid agony" of Hamlet. The unfortunate perpetrator of the "bull" escaped with a sarcastic editorial reference in the next issue to the "intelligent compositor" who could not dissociate the ideas of "solidity" and "agony." But the ridicule of the thing preyed on the poor fellow's mind and set him a-roving. That was more than thirty years ago, and when I last heard from him he was still expiating his error by the "solid agony" of "hitting the road."

Fortunately for themselves, the majority of compositors are less sensitive than the one just mentioned, for there are few indeed who would not plead guilty to some more or less ridiculous "bull" at some time in the course of their experience. The best of printers were liable to these humiliating accidents. Probably more common, everyday errors are to be found in the machine-set papers of the present, but for a real, laughable and at the same time exasperating "bull," the unreasoning machine is not "in it" with the elaborate perversity of a "pied" brained compositor. Consider, for instance, the fiendish ingenuity amounting almost to genius of the artist who rendered the advice of Hamlet to Horatio to "crook the pregnant hinges of the knee that thrift may follow fawning," as "creak the fragrant hinges of the gate that theft may follow forgery." A somewhat stilted writer on a prominent Western paper who was fond of airing bits of classic lore was horrified one morning to see a neat reference to the moral lesson the ancient Spartans drew from the drunken Helots utterly ruined by the typographical transmogrification of the unhappy Helots into "drunken harlots." The writer fumed and tore around after the scalp of the guilty comp., who took the matter very coolly and justified himself by saying that he had never seen a drunken Helot, but he had seen many a drunken harlot, and he insisted to the raging writer that moral lesson was as good in the latter case as the former. He made out a defense entirely to his own satisfaction, but, nevertheless, he was released from further service on that paper, and betook himself to his travels, but very far from being haunted by the Nemesis of his "bull," is very prone to tell the story as an instance of a very natural mistake on the part of a compositor and the unreasonable anger of a "thin-skinned dude writer."

Opie Read

OPIE PERCIVAL READ (1852–1939) was born in Nashville and died in Chicago. By the time he was 35 he had edited five Southern papers and then started *The Arkansas Traveler*, a humor magazine. After moving to Chicago in 1897 he published 31 novels (some like *The Starbucks*, 1902, were written in Southern dialect), 18 short story collections and five works of nonfiction. He is first to have put the phrase, attributed to P. T. Barnum, "There's a sucker born every minute," into print. His novel *Old Ebenezer* (Chicago, Laird & Lee, 1897) has a shady printer called Lyman in it, always trying to scam money out of folks. Hurry up, he urges a client, I've got a tramp printer waiting for the copy. Later Lyman says, "I paid the tramp thirty cents for his time and he has gone away happier than if he had been put to work." Barney the tramp printer we are about to meet appears in this novel also:

> "The picturesque old philosopher known as the tramp printer is only a memory now," said Lyman. "I have seen him strolling along the road, sore of foot, stubble-faced, almost ragged, hungry, but with a cynical head full of contempt for the man of regular habits. I recall one particularly — Barney Caldwell."
> "What?" cried Hillit, raising upon his elbows, "did you know old

Barney? He was once foreman of an office in Cincinnati where I was a cub. He was comparatively young then, but they called him the old man. And what a disciplinarian! He used to say, 'Boys, if you get drunk with me it is your own look out, and if you don't walk the chalk line that's my look out. Don't expect favors, because you happen to be a good fellow.' One day, he came into the office, and after starting to put on his apron he hesitated, and turning to a fellow named Hicks, he said: 'Charley, I've a notion to be a gentleman once more.' Then I heard a man standing near me say: 'There'll be a vacant foremanship in this office within five minutes. The old man is going to take to the road.' And he did. He resigned his position and walked out. Life was worth living in those days, Mr. Lyman."

In "The Incense of Chicken" we encounter the braggadocio of printers proud of being swift — in this case impossibly fast — typesetters, who would hope to clear out their galley and get a fat take of ad copy. There's a great anonymous poem in the 1893 Cleveland Type Foundry specimen book that captures this competitiveness:

KNOCKED OUT

He skimmed the case at a lively pace, and ever anon his look surveyed with the fire of keen desire, the copy-burdened hook. And swift and sly, his wary eye each comrade's copy scanned, for it was no sin the "ad" to win by the speed of his good right hand.

Old Barney

STANDING AT HIS OFFICE WINDOW, many a man looks out upon a scene of turmoil, and wonders what has become of a certain tramp printer whom he knew years ago. I have one in mind. I remember many, for they strolled with the seasons, northward and southward, keeping pace with the varying moods of the year; but one of them stands bold and clear in the vivid light of the long ago. I can see his sun-burned face, his stubbed red beard — always about six weeks old — his blue eyes, dimmed by many a gas-light; I can catch the accent of his cynical utterances. He held man in contempt, but would share his last bit of tobacco with him. Woman stood beyond the border line of his consideration, but in his pocket he carried the faded and mouse-gnawed photograph of a girl. He always entered the office with a limp, with a tip-tap of his worn-down shoes. The boys were ever glad to see him, for he brought many a new story, and our welcome of him was loud and hearty. He was modest in his responses — merely nodded at our enthusiasm. His name was Barney Fugerson.

One night, upon a spread of newspapers, he lay in the office. All day he had distributed "tight" advertisements and dead time-tables. He filled his pipe with three or four grades of tobacco and began to talk.

"Why don't you boys apprentice yourselves to a butcher and learn to hack off meat?" he asked.

"Oh, you want to be printers, eh? Too many at the business already. Better learn to hack off beef."

"Do you wish that you had learned it?" I ventured to ask.

He turned over on his side, gave me a full view of his blurred eyes and thus answered: "No, for my case was hopeless from the start. Give me a match."

I brought him a match. He lighted his pipe and lay on his back, puffing and looking up at the smoke. How I envied him, his skill at the case, his knowledge of the world. He was a great man berating the means that had made him great.

"Oh, I know you boys think that you would improve on my condition," said he, but you wouldn't. You'd be homeless just as I am."

"But why should you be homeless?" I asked.

Again he gave me a full view of his blurred eyes. "Because my blood is too quick," he answered. "It would be impossible for me to settle down and live as other men do. Prosperity would wear me out. Three meals a day and a place to sleep would weigh on my mind and eventually kill me. But I can't tramp always," he added with a sigh. "One of these days I'll be compelled to hold a regular sit. You boys will wonder why old Barney does not come round and the years will pass and you will see him not. And then you will forget him."

We cried out that we could never forget him. "Oh, yes, you will," he persisted. We were strong in our protests against this unjust opinion. He sighed distressfully, and taking out an empty half-pint bottle, said: "If you think you won't, prove it by getting this bottle filled with corn-juice. See if you can raise enough money among you."

We grabbled out all the money we had, and the bottle was filled. Then he told us of his work on the great daily papers and we sat entranced. We learned that the foremen in all great printing houses were wolves and that all editors were ignorant. He had taken the twist out of many a sentence written by men of national reputation. He took out a copy of the *Courier-Journal* and pointed out matter that he had set up, telegraphed from Russia, and we read it over and over again. He produced a soiled cutting, an editorial from the *New York Tribune*, and informed us that he had put it in type from original manuscript. We asked him if it were Greeley's writing and he answered that it was not. "Bone Smith and Jay Cloyd set up the old man's stuff," said he. "I think this thing was written by Dana."

"Was it hard to read?" one of the boys asked.

"Not for me. But a blacksmith couldn't have made out a word of it."

"Did you ever strike anything you couldn't read?" I asked.

"Did I? I was in Cincinnati not long ago and they stood me up against some of old Bloss; and I rattled an em-quad in a stick, put on my coat and left town. Hadn't gone very far before I overtook Oscar Howard. Asked him why he had left so suddenly and he simply said 'Bloss.' That was enough and we shook hands."

"But how about Watterson's matter?"

"Oh, he wabbles, but he's easy."

"Does anybody write correctly?"

"Haven't found him. Once in a while an old printer quits the case and takes to the pen; and naturally enough he writes fairly well."

"But the foremen can't write anything, can they?"

"Not a line."

He had helped to set up the sermons of the great preachers in the East, had worked on the *New York Ledger*, and he showed us a "take" of "Norwood," the novel written by Beecher. He halted so often in his discourse to "nip" the bottle that his pipe was constantly going out, and he kept us busy striking matches for him. I knew that he could write a greater story than "Norwood" or Sylvanus Cobb's "Gunmaker of Moscow," and I asked him why he didn't. His pipe was out again and I lighted a match for him and held it over the blackened bowl.

"Why — don't — I? That'll do. Thank you. Why don't I? Well, the fact is, I haven't had time. But somebody ought to do something in the literary line. Those fellows can't write — can't even spell."

I was sorry to hear this, for the "Gunmaker of Moscow" had delighted me and I had read it time and again, believing each time that Cobb was surely the world's greatest writer, and wondering why kings and queens did not leap down from their thrones to grasp his hand. But Barney Fugerson said that he could not write. It was a struggle, but I was forced to acknowledge within the darkening sanctuary of my literary estimate that he couldn't.

It was late when we left him lying there on his pallet of papers, with a lamp burning on a corner of the imposing stone just above his head. Reluctantly I bade him good-night — I would willingly have sat with him until sunrise — and went to my bed to muse over his modest and self-repressing genius. I dreamed of him, dreamed that the world had at last acknowledged his greatness and that he had not denied me a friendly nod. Early at morning I hastened to the office to sweep out and to put a bucket of fresh water in the "sanctum." Barney was gone. He had rolled up his bed and taken it with him, not to sleep upon but to read by the roadside.

Nearly a year passed before I saw him again. And he came back the very afternoon that the black martins returned to build their nests under the eaves of the Methodist church. The office had changed hands; a lawyer had bought the paper; mine was the only familiar face. Barney came in with his tip-tap, spread out a copy of the paper to see whether any contemptuous change had been effected in the style of the paper, turned to me and in an undertone said: "They've made a horse-bill out of it. Too many stud heads. Lawyer owns it now, eh? He can't write. Good-bye."

And so he left. I have never seen him since that afternoon when the black martins were building their nests under the eaves of the Methodist church. I sit and look out on a scene of turmoil, and I wonder what ever became of old Barney.

The Incense of Chicken

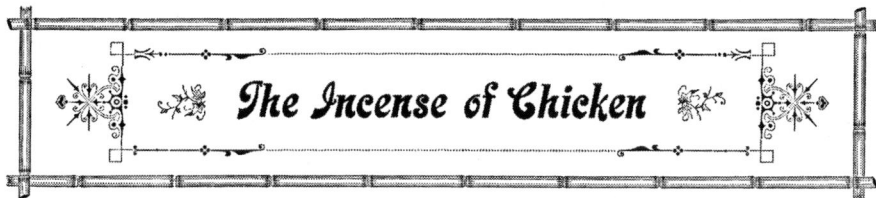

A STROKE OF MISFORTUNE made me one of the owners of
the paper. I had set type in the office, and for my accumulat-
ed string I accepted stock. The sheet was known (limited) as
the *Evening Mail,* and was published in Nashville, Tennessee.
The Centennial at Philadelphia was striving to pour balm on
the slow-healing war-wounds of the country. But Nast's tiger*
still crouched in the political jungle, and the bloody shirt had
been washed through but one water. It was at such a time that
our paper preached sermons of brotherly love, written by an
old gentleman whom we paid, or agreed to pay, $5 a week. In
terms of tenderness he referred to our hated contemporary,
a pirate whose insulting steam was always up, and who was
constantly driving its iron ram into our vulnerable parts. One
day the brotherly sheriff came in and showed his strong attach-
ment for us. We closed our volume with an editorial entitled
"The Whole Duty of Man." In the town there were more printers than work. Circumstances, the most peremptory of physi-
cians, advised a change of scene. Bob Dutton, who had received
similar advice, went with me. We tramped. I was young and
inclined to tell truth. I don't know whether Bob lied because he

---

* Nast's tiger = German-born Thomas Nast was the major political cartoon-
ist of the period of Reconstruction after the Civil War. He broke the corrup-
tion of New York politics with his satires of "Boss" Tweed and the Tammany
Tiger, representing the voracious Democrats who controlled city hall. He
created the donkey and elephant symbols of the political parties, as well as
the popular image of a jolly, fat bearded Santa Claus and the original Uncle
Sam.

had no conscience or whether he desperately choked the truth to kill his conscience, feeling that he was hampered by it. In the army he had been punished for stealing a barrel of whisky from an officer who had stolen it. There is no greater crime than to steal from a thief. Peace settled upon the country and disgrace fell upon Bob at about the same time. I was warned not to take him as a traveling companion, but in the warning there was a hint at adventure, and this, of course, sweetened his disreputable company. We wandered off down into the cypress country of West Tennessee, dodging high water on our way to Memphis. We were constantly cut off from our supplies. "I may not amount to much in a general way," Bob would declare, "but I've got an appetite sharp enough to shave with."

Late one afternoon we came to a cabin set on a sandy knoll, in the thick shade of scrub oaks. A red-whiskered man stood in the door. We asked for something to eat. He appeared pleased to see us.

"Come in," he said. "Sit down there. Where are you from and what is your line of employment when you so far forget yourselves as to work?"

This rascally insinuation pleased Bob. "We are printers," said he.

"That so? Do you mean that you make newspapers?"

"Well, we do the only work of any importance. We set the type, and the other features do not amount to anything."

"So you set the type." And then, calling to a woman, he commanded: "Jane, kill two of those young dominecker chickens for these gentlemen, and fry them brown."

Bob's eyes snapped, and I felt an emotional surge of water in my mouth. For days we had fed upon the tasteless berry of the swamp, and the leathery "hand-out" passed from the kitchen window. We had dreamed even of fat bacon. Our cowed souls had not dared to muse upon fried chicken. Bob strove to say something, but emotion overcame him. We heard the chickens flutter — heard the axe fall upon their necks.

"So you set type," said the host, stroking his beard. "Is there much money in such work?"

"Fortunes," Bob answered, with a stir of his lying impulse. "But the trouble is that work is hard to get. It is a sort of luxury."

"Do they pay you by the newspaper you set up or by the week?"

"By the piece," Bob answered.

"I don't exactly understand," said the host, pondering. "How by the piece?"

"Why, by the em. We get so much a thousand ems."

"But suppose you set up something that hasn't many m's in it? Then you don't get much pay. It don't strike me that this is a very good arrangement."

Bob laughed pityingly. "Why, it is measured by the space that so many ems would occupy."

"Oh, I understand now. And the faster a man is the more money he gets; it doesn't make any difference whether he picks up real m's or not."

"Yes, sir; that's the idea."

The redolence of frying chicken floated through the door, an incense burnt upon the memory-altar of youth.

"Well," said the host, "about how many ems can you set in a day?"

No incense could have kept Bob from lying at this moment. "Let me see," he said, seeming to search his memory, "I reckon I can set about twenty-five thousand."

"That so?"

"That's a fact. Ain't it?" he asked, turning to me. It's singular, but a man rarely has the nerve to refuse testimony to a lie. We were called upon for proof. "Ain't that so, Bill?" It is so easy to say yes; it saves dissension. I said "yes."

"And about how much a thousand do you get?" the host asked.

"Seventy-five cents or a dollar. Ain't that so?"

I said "yes."

"Well, you ought to make money at that," he said, and looking at him I saw something that froze my blood. He had taken a printer's make-up rule from his pocket, this red-headed man of the wilderness — had taken out a make-up rule and was cleaning his finger nails with it. Bob saw this dreadful sight. He caught his breath. He said nothing. He snatched his hat and was gone. I couldn't stay — I had stood god-father to his lie. The chicken incense followed us mockingly down into the woods and there left us. We heard a rooster crow. We heard the laugh of the red-bearded man.

SMITH

SOME TWENTY-TWO YEARS AGO I was running a country printing office in Connecticut, in the easy old-fashioned way before
the inroads of city dailies had obliged the country editors to
bestir themselves and get up really newsy papers. One day a
round-shouldered, long-moustached and bedraggled tramp
printer walked into the office, marched straight up to a high
stool standing in the middle of the floor, and seated himself
with the simple remark: "I'm tired." He did not tell any of us
that he was a printer. We knew it by the frayed condition of
his pantaloons and the unwashed shirt that peeped necktieless
through the top opening of the faded broadcloth coat that he
wore. He saw that he was sized up, and he also recognized intuitively by the easy way in which we took things that no rush
of work existed in the office. Presently he opened out in the
style of an accomplished orator, with full, complete and correct
enunciation of every word:

"Gentlemen, I have just walked over from Meriden. I have
not had a day's work since I left Albany. I have tramped, and
begged, and slept on piles of waste paper. I am footsore and I'm
starving. For God's sake give me a chance to work my fingers
and rest my feet. I don't want any money, but I do need some
square meals, some clean clothes and a place where I can get a
decent night's sleep."

The appeal was more than I could stand. I sent him first to
the sink and then to the restaurant, after which he threw in a

case of type. I took him home with me that night and gave him some clean clothes and a comfortable straw bed in the attic. He was the first one up in the house next morning, skirmished around and built the kitchen fire and had coffee made and the breakfast nearly ready when the family turned out. His manners were those of a polished gentleman, and his housework superior to that of any servant maid I ever saw.

He remained with me three months, during which time he was general handy man everywhere. He would write editorials or turn press with equal cheerfulness. He was a slow but correct compositor and a tasteful jobber. In my absence he estimated on jobs and managed customers with all possible tact. He entertained all hands by his brilliant conversation and inimitable story-telling abilities. He did half the housework at my home and played chess with me evenings. He never asked for any money, but occasionally requested that the devil have ten cents to purchase for him a chew of tobacco.

But the help required in my office was small, and I did not really require him, nor was I able to dispense with anyone in order to make a place for Smith, as I will call our tramping friend. So one day I suggested to him that he was now rested, and clean and well clothed, and if he would advertise in the nearest city or look in at the offices, a man of his capacity would not be long in obtaining work at a salary commensurate with his abilities. He thanked me, and said he supposed it was time to move on. I told him that there was no hurry, but that I could not keep him permanently, and gave him twenty-five dollars and suggested that he go to Meriden, Hartford and New Haven and look in at all the leading offices, and if he found nothing, come back and wait until something should develop. So he shook hands all around, and departed, as we supposed, for Meriden.

Two days later I heard of him, through our devil. Said he, "Smith's at Blank's saloon, drunk as a lord; been there ever since he left here." I made up my mind to go and rescue him as soon as I could leave the office, but shortly before six he came stumbling in, very dirty and very drunk. He wanted to lie down on a pile of paper and go to sleep, and we let him. Next morning when the force turned up at the office Smith was minus, and so were a pair of almost new shoes and a gold pen. The surmise that Smith had taken these and pawned them for liquor to continue his drunk proved correct. I made a vain effort to sober up the man that night, but it was no use; the next morning he was off with some more minor articles, which he pawned for more liquor. Then I called in an officer, and Smith was led away and was afterward brought before the court and sent to the county jail for sixty days.

Just twenty-eight days later I had a letter from him stating that the county commissioners were to hold a meeting in two days, and that they had authority to pardon him. He thought he had been punished enough, and that if I, the complainant, wrote to them he would be released. I wrote the letter as requested, and two days later in walked Smith, very tired and dusty, but thankful to be again among friends. He did not even ask to be set to work, but just wiped his brow, got a drink of water, hung up his coat on his old nail, took some copy off the hook and began setting type. I had not the heart to turn him off, and he worked away for another three months, once more the gentlemanly, hard-working and happy Smith.

He told us more of his own history this time. He had been secretary for General Butler during the war, and had been editor and part owner of a flourishing paper in New York State for a year and a half, a member of the Congregational Church, and recognized as one of the leading men of the town. But he could not resist the tendency to go on a tremendous drunk every few months, and this was his ruin. He stayed with me several months longer, when I sold the office, and he went in one direction, I in another. Six months later he wrote me from

Syracuse, saying that he had a comfortable place, though the pay was only nine dollars. I answered this letter but he wrote no more.

Ten years afterwards I was running a job-printing office in a town in south Jersey, and one afternoon who should walk in but Smith, as footworn and weary, and ragged and dirty as when I first met him. He was immensely glad to see me, and after a half hour's talk over things which we had in common, he took off his coat, as if he were employed, and said, "What shall I do?" I liked him too well to give him the cold shoulder, and set him to work cleaning out cases. At night he followed me home, and resumed his old place as maid-of-all-work.

I really had no employment for him in the office, but kept him around for a week or so, and then got him a place on a morning daily newspaper, printed in the next building. He went on as ad. setter, and vastly improved the paper, taking his own time to re-set old ads that looked slovenly, and inside of a month the whole character of the paper was improved. He then worked into a reportorial position, did two men's work right along, and did it well. He became the proprietor's right-hand man, and received a fair salary — on paper. He asked the proprietor to keep his salary, telling him frankly that he could not trust himself with money.

Things went on swimmingly for several months, and Smith began to be known all over town as a bright newspaper man and a great hustler, who was just the making of the *Morning Primrose*. But the culmination I feared came in due course. One evening I went into the *Primrose* office and found the proprietor hustling out copy, doing Smith's work, while Smith lay around maudlin drunk. I put him in a hack and took him to my home and sobered him up. Next day he was very penitent, and in the afternoon he returned to his work, but only for one day. The following day he was hopelessly drunk again. He drew all his back salary, and when that was gone discovered that his position gave him credit in every saloon in town, and that he could hang them up for as much as he pleased.

The drunk lasted a week or longer, and there was no doing anything with Smith. He only escaped arrest because every one of the police knew him personally and liked him. He kept coming into the *Primrose* office in a "boozy" condition and interfering with business, until the proprietor, a real good fellow, could stand it no longer, and came to me, saying, "I'll have to get rid of Smith some way. He just ruins my business, coming in drunk and trying to talk to advertisers. Will you chip in with me and pay his fare to New York? He has drawn all his savings and blown in every dollar." I said I would, and we sent for a hackman, giving him twenty-five cents to take Smith to the station and money to buy a ticket to New York, with instructions to put the ticket in Smith's pocket and see him on the train. He did so, and we sighed and thought that was the last of Smith. But not quite. A week later I received a letter from a brother in New York informing me that Smith had come to him, confessed that he had been on a drunk and was shipped out of town to save his reputation, and being now sobered, desired money to return, where his old position remained waiting for him. He got the fare, but returned again two days later, to confess that he had spent it in drink, and to beg for just one more trial, saying that this time he would surely go back to his work. My brother told him, "You're no man at all. There's half a dollar. Never let me see you again."

And that is the last I ever heard of poor Smith, the most brilliant tramp printer I ever knew, who would have been an ornament to any society and a conspicuous man in any circle if he could have resisted his appetite for ruin. I believe he belonged to a well-to-do family, but had worn the patience of all his relatives before he came in my way. Perhaps he is now dead; perhaps he has reformed, perhaps he is still tramping.

BEANBODY

ABOUT 1885 THE WRITER started a daily paper, with morning, evening and Sunday editions, in a New Jersey town, and while engaged in excavating the cellar to make a foundation for the fast press which was to turn out the papers, a tramp printer walked in on me with a request for a job. Being a little short of help for the morning edition, I hired him to work nights, at his own figure, nine dollars a week, he explaining that while he was really a fifteen-dollar man, he was willing to work for that price three months, while we were getting under way. His name was Beanbody, and I turned him loose in the cellar, and he did odd jobs very efficiently for a couple of days. Then the type came in, and I let him lay all the cases. After starting on the job, he came to me and inquired whether there were any peculiarities in the local method of laying out the cases, as they ought to be laid like those in neighboring offices. I was struck with the good sense and judgment that prompted the suggestion, and sent him to a near-by job printer's to copy the lay of his cases. I was afterward satisfied that his real anxiety to know the lay of the cases in the surrounding offices was that he did not feel at all sure where the odd sorts belonged, and was even a little shy on exclamation points, brackets, etc. Having got a copy of the cases from the job printer's he was all right, and finished the work in good shape. In the meantime he had done several other things that increased my confidence, and as a result, when we started up, Beanbody was put in as night foreman, in the composing room.

Of course, what with morning, evening and Sunday editions,

the office was open almost all the time, and although Bean-body was on duty only from 7 p.m. to 4 a.m., yet he was always about the office for five or six hours in the daytime, sleeping on a cot in an adjoining room, and getting up shortly before noon. He turned half reporter and general handy man after-noons, and made himself most serviceable. As a result, inside of two weeks, I found that I had made myself responsible for his board, given him an order on a tailor for about thirty dol-lars, and on a furniture man for his cot and bedding, so that he was considerably ahead of me, notwithstanding the amount of overtime he was making. About this time I complained to the night compositors, in the absence of Beanbody, that they did not get up as much type as ought to be set by their number, and one of them spoke up and said that he always had to do the bulk of the making up, as Beanbody did not know how, and another said that Beanbody did not set over two or three stick-fuls a night, besides which he simply took the proofs and sat around and bossed the others. This did not look well, and I told Beanbody that in future I expected him to do the entire mak-ing up. The next morning the paper was two hours late, and it was the worst made-up sheet I ever saw. Beanbody had made it up all alone, as none of the men would help him, and some of the columns were filled out with half a dozen leads between the type and the foot slug, and others were solid up against the head rule, a few headings were misplaced, one head rule was turned about, and the entire job was terribly bungled. In addi-tion, the pressman told me that they would not have got out at all, if he had not jammed up the last two forms and made them lift after a fashion, and so got them on the press.

This could not go on, so I took Beanbody off the night force and put him on the case with the day force, and called him as-sistant foreman to alleviate his feelings, which were very much hurt by the come-down. About this time our young lady clerk and bookkeeper left, and Beanbody recommended a young woman from his boarding place. I told him to send her around. She came the next day, while I was away, and, as Beanbody informed me when I got back, "she offered to work so cheap, three dollars a week, that I hired her and set her to work." I was not particularly impressed with the girl's appearance, or by the small value she placed on her services, but I decided to give her a week's trial. On her second day I found her sitting in a fine new armchair, and Beanbody informed me that he thought it was a pity for her to sit on a hard chair, so he had bought her a comfortable one. She proved very inefficient, and at the close of the week I let her go. This was a sad blow to Beanbody, who argued with me to retain her, but without effect, as he was not in much favor with me at this time, owing to some further developments as to his workmanship. The day foreman told me that he did not set more than three thousand ems a day, and that his proof was dirty at that. Beanbody was now owing me about twenty dollars, and I was anxious to get it worked out and let him go. One day he distributed a column of live type, and I happened to be the one to discover it, and found fault with him before all the composing room. He went right for his coat, and declared that he would not work any longer for a man that would abuse him, after the way he had slaved night and day to put the paper on its feet. I called him out into the office and expostulated with him, and asked him if that was a proper return to make me after my advancing him clothes, etc., to go away twenty dollars in my debt. "Don't think I'd be so dishonorable as not to pay it," he exclaimed. "I will send you half the money I earn until the whole sum is settled."

I suggested that it would be more sensible and proper for him to work for me, as the work was there, and he finally agreed to go on by the piece, and work off the score. His first week on the case by the piece netted him five dollars and fifty cents, and he tried several ingenious methods of getting back on a weekly salary, but I was sick of him, and paid no attention. Finally, he came to my house about five o'clock one morning, and called me out of bed in the most urgent fashion. I supposed that there had been a murder or something, and that there was a demand for an extra, and tumbling out, got dressed in a jiffy, and let him in.

"If you please, Mr. Thomas," he said, "I am in an awful scrape. I'm being sued for breach of promise, and I hear that a warrant is out for my arrest, and I want you, please, to let me have two dollars to get out of town. There is about eight dollars due on my string so far this week, and I'll leave you that handsome armchair I bought for the girl bookkeeper, and that will about square us."

I laughed in his face and said: "Why should anybody sue you, Beanbody? Can't they see that you never have a cent?"

"Oh, I have money coming to me when my father dies," he replied, "and they know it, and so have planned to trap me. If you'll let me have the two dollars it will pay my fare to Trenton, and they won't know where to place me."

Having about come to the conclusion that it would be a good thing to get rid of Beanbody at any price I gave him the two dollars and bade him travel. The next morning I found that the two dollars I had given him fully covered what was his due for the type he had set that week. Next his landlady called on me and said that I owed her between six and seven dollars for Beanbody's board for eleven days. Expostulations were of no avail. I had endorsed him and sent her a note, and I had to pay it all. On the first of the month following I received a bill from my next door neighbor, the furniture man, for ten dollars for the armchair. I went in and told him that I had bought no armchair. He replied that my foreman had purchased it and charged it to me. He had just promised me an advertisement, so I had to let it go in payment of that.

When I settled up with the clothing man who had fitted out Beanbody I found that he had trusted him with six dollars' worth more of goods the day before he skipped, and although he admitted he could not make me pay for them, as I had only given an order on him for thirty dollars, yet he said that he had trusted him because he was my foreman, and that if I turned such people loose on a community I ought to be responsible, and as he was a good advertiser I thought it wiser to pay the amount than to quarrel with him about it.

Nor was this all. Beanbody actually eloped with the poor girl whom he had hired for me as bookkeeper, married her, and took her tramping with him. She came back home in about three months, much wiser and sadder, but subsequently, I believe, succeeded in having her marriage annulled, and it is to be hoped found a better husband next time.

Yet once more was I destined to hear of Beanbody. About a year later a fellow publisher in a neighboring city wrote me that he had recently taken on a new foreman, who brought a letter of recommendation from me, but he turned out to be so incompetent that he had been obliged to dispense with him. The publisher was curious to know how I came to recommend him. He received a letter of sympathy, but in this case I declined to make good the damage, as the letter of recommendation was of course a forgery.

MORNINGSTAR

"I'M MOST FROZE."

Such was the brief utterance with which Emanuel Morning-star greeted the devil of the Patriot Press office in Shohock-en about seven o'clock one morning in 1876. The hands were not yet on duty, as this was a place where the proprietor never came down before a quarter of eight in the morning, hence the foreman made his time between seven-twenty and seven-thirty, while the compositors and press boy found that a quarter past seven was soon enough to make sure of being at work when the foreman arrived. As the devil had to sweep up and fix the fires before the rest arrived he was usually there at seven, and on this occasion he had found a tramp printer on the step awaiting the opening of the door.

Having thawed himself out, and made various flippant remarks to the several hands as they came in, by way of amusing them and securing their good will, Emanuel secured a stick, and when the foreman came in he was putting in the type at a rapid rate.

"Good morning, Mr. Boss," said Emanuel. "I'm just taking the stiffening out of my fingers."

A moment later he brought his stick and laid it in front of the foreman, who read the following:

> I am young
> With no part to my hair,
> And not fair,
> And trousers much frayed at the bottom;
> I can set
> Up more type
> 'Twixt dark and daylight
> Than any old comp. in Shohocken.

"Set and composed in exactly four minutes by the devil's Waterbury. Isn't that good for fifteen cents to buy me a breakfast?"

The foreman thought that it was, or at least he produced the money, and Morningstar, whose name was either assumed or a translation from the German, shot out for some grub. In half an hour he was back begging for a case, and as there happened to be a little rush in the office he was put on. He slapped up more type that day than had ever been done before in the history of the office, and kept up the pace all the week, sleeping on a pile of paper in the corner of the pressroom, and begging fifty cents each night for meals. After about the third day the editor and proprietor of the *Patriot*, which was a country daily, began to find a bunch of news items on the desk each morning, which Morningstar had gathered the evening before, in lounging about the neighboring general stores. They were useful, and inside of two weeks the proprietor volunteered to give Morningstar an order for some presentable clothes, in order that he might use him to report other and more important matters.

The man developed so fast, and made himself so useful, that the proprietor found himself wondering one day what was the matter with Morningstar, that he had come to town in such a forlorn condition, when he was such a valuable acquisition to the office. He had not long to find out. One day he was called by urgent political business to the county seat, and told Morningstar to run in a couple of more columns of locals, leaving him virtually in editorial charge for the rest of the day. That evening, on his return, he purchased a copy of his paper on the train, and had not read very far before he struck this item:

> "Zwiggs & Blout, the new meat men, are hustlers, and may always
> be found on duty at No. 2 Warren street."

This read all right to a stranger, but as our editor knew that

No. 2 Warren street was not where the young meat men belonged, but the address of a saloon of very bad repute, he swore softly to himself, and read on. Pretty soon he struck this:

> "Now is the time to die. Perkins is giving cut price funerals, and will bury people at bargain prices all through the holidays."

The couple in the seat behind the editor were astonished at this point to hear the strength of the forcible expletives that came from the gentlemanly appearing man with the *Patriot* in his hand. They had not long to wait for a further outburst of smothered exasperation, as this met the editor's eye:

> "Geo. H. Downing's hencoop took fire at 3.15 this morning, and the entire department was called out to smother the flames. George himself turned out, *en robe du nuit,* and saved two tender young pullets and a bantam rooster."

It happened that Downing was a most staid old gentle man, of high standing, wealthy, and the holder of a mortgage on the Patriot Press. Naturally, the editor groaned, and wondered vaguely how it had happened that such things got into his paper, and whether he should ever be able to make it right with the people attacked by the practical joker who seemed to have taken charge, for there were a dozen more items of the same character in the columns on that unfortunate day.

On arriving at Shohocken he went straight to the house of his foreman, to demand an explanation. He found that worthy very anxious to explain. It appeared that Morningstar had set up a half a galley of items, written by himself, and of which he had read his own proof and then assisted the foreman in the make-up. As a consequence no one else had read the dreadful lot of practical jokes until the whole edition was printed and on the street. One of the compositors had then called his attention to the matter, and he had remonstrated with Morningstar, who seemed to think that it was a mighty good joke, and to be rather surprised that anybody should take it seriously.

Of course Morningstar was lectured, paid off, and discharged. Nothing else could have appeased the wrath of the patrons of the *Patriot*. His youth was no excuse, and out he went. The editor had found out what was the matter with his hustling young workman, and that he had a blind, unreasoning desire to play practical jokes. There was one man in Shohocken, however, who appreciated the funny side of the matter. That was the publisher of the rival sheet, who had looked with some envy upon the *Patriot's* acquisition of the bright young printer and reporter. He sent for Morningstar the next day, gave him a long talk of fatherly advice, and put him to work on the *Bugle*, first stipulating that as a penance he should go about and personally apologize to every man who considered himself insulted by the jokes in the *Patriot*. Morningstar did so, and, what is more, profited by the lesson. In a few years he became foreman of the *Bugle*; later a partner, and still later proprietor. Four years ago the *Patriot* was for sale, and Morningstar bought the concern, and now runs the consolidated *Bugle-Patriot*, and conducts a large job printing establishment, serving the public with satisfaction. He has been mayor of Shohocken, and served in the Legislature of his State. He is not ashamed to allow it to be known that he was once a tramp printer, but rather takes a pride in having it known that he is entirely a self-made man. He tells the comps that he is still the fastest type-slinger in Shohocken, and while they shake their heads at this they cannot disprove the statement, as Morningstar never sets any type nowadays, and his record of some 17,000 ems within ten hours remains unbroken in Shohocken to this day.

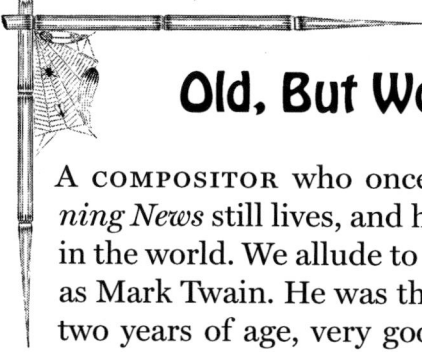

Old, But Worth Repeating.

A COMPOSITOR who once worked on the St. Louis *Evening News* still lives, and has since made considerable stir in the world. We allude to Samuel Clemens, better known as Mark Twain. He was then about twenty-one or twenty-two years of age, very good-looking, and most intensely impressed with that fact. He was the laziest mortal that ever "soldiered"* on the hook. In that year (1855) the Crimean war and the printers were raging — the latter over the long, diabolical combination of consonants that made up the Russian officers' names. When a steamer arrived at New York, the telegraph would fire these infernal hard names over the wires until the tops of the posts were shattered to pieces. Sam Clemens used to say that the operator never wrote these names; when he came to a hard name, he just took up a pepper-box of black-lead and shook it over the manuscript. Sam was known to dwell for fifteen minutes over a Russian name, and then to snatch a few z's, three &'s, and then, fencing them with an ! he would go ahead until the first galley came around to allow him a rest. He occupied a stand in the corner of the room, which had been christened "Sebastopol." After the paper went to press, all the old shoes, loose quoins, etc., would be gathered up, and then the entire force would storm "Sebastopol." Sam would dodge around pretty lively until the enemy had exhausted their ammunition, when he would make a sortie and repay them with interest.

Sam was lazy; he had a peculiar manner of drawling out his words that was irresistibly comic when relating a joke

---

* "Soldier" or "sojer" = to finesse for a better take (Levenson).

or something; but he was good-hearted and good-natured, and much liked. One hot morning in June, Sam did not make his appearance until about nine o'clock, when he ought to have been there promptly at seven. The foreman (Mr. John F. Bailey) was excited and angry; and as Sam came sauntering slowly in, languidly fanning himself with his straw hat, Bailey said, "—! —! —! it, Sam, if you can't get here before this time of day you needn't come at all." Sam leaned upon the imposing-stone with both elbows, and faintly drawled out, "Well — John —I — guess —I —won't — come — egin; it's — too — d-----d — hot!" And he slowly meandered out of the composing room.

That was the last of Sam Clemens' type-setting. He got a berth on the river, became a pilot, & — Mark Twain. The world knows the rest.

~~~~~~

LEGISLATIVE PROCEEDINGS.
House — Third Day.

Carson, January 14.

[Say — you have got a compositor up there who is too rotten particular, it seems to me. When I spell "devil" in my usual frank and open manner, he puts it "d——l!" Now, Lord love his conceited and accommodating soul, if I choose to use the language of the vulgar, the low-flung and the sinful, and such as will shock the ears of the highly civilized I don't want him to appoint himself an editorial critic and proceed to tone me down and save me from the consequences of my conduct; that is, unless I pay him for it, which I won't. I expect I could spell "devil" before that fastidious cuss was born. — Mark Twain]

The Speaker called the house to order at 10 a.m. ...

WILLIAM ADAMS

WILLIAM E. ADAMS (1832–1906), known as a Chartist, radical and journalist, was for a long time the editor of the Newcastle *Weekly Chronicle*. John Savile says of him, "He was greatly respected in social and political circles in the Northeast, although it was Adams of the Dicky Bird Society [which promoted the protection of birds and suppressed egg collecting and the use of feathers in millinery] they remembered rather than the author of the 1858 pamphlet on Tyrannicide." In 1900 he retired to Madeira to write his memoirs.

Apprenticed to a printer, J. J. Hadley of the Cheltenham *Journal* in 1846, Adams's first duties were to ink small bill formes and deliver the papers. Blistered hands came from one operation, blistered feet from the other.

Adams was a disciple of Mazzini, a staunch Republican, "but not a Red Republican." From 1854–5 he printed *The English Republic* from a mansion on Coniston Water in the Lake District. He was the compositor and Thomas Hailing (later a renowned printer in Cheltenham) was the pressman.

Hailing wrote an autobiographical sketch for *The British Printer* (vol. II, no. 7, January 1889). He recalled:

At eight years of age my "education" was finished, and I took the degree of P.D. [*i.e. Printer's Devil*] in my grandfather's office at Cheltenham, where, mounted upon *two* type-boxes, I was introduced to the art and mystery of rolling at a folio press, and after a plentiful crop of blisters on my hands and a disreputable acquaintance with sundry "monks" and "friars," I was drafted off to help my uncle who had set up as a printer at Gloucester. He hit upon the novel idea of working all night, so that we could have a rare lot of holidays in the daytime! And then we had sailing matches on the river that flowed around the old city walls, games at quoits, archery, etc. "In these delightful pleasant groves" we were not privileged, however, to remain long: our talents were not appreciated, and the shutters were put up one quarter-day.

In 1852 he went to Coniston to "take charge of a small office started by Mr. W. J. Linton, the celebrated engraver," and there he met Adams and printed the *English Republic* and the *Northern Tribune*. "These two magazines lived about two years, and this period marks the happiest days of my life and of all others concerned." The house was later bought by Ruskin, who tore it down. After the paper expired Hailing moved to Windermere and wrought on the writings of Harriet Martineau, who thought she was dying and therefore wanted her autobiography set in type. "This was in 1855; but the careful authoress lived for two-and-twenty years after she had brought her book to a conclusion! Creaking doors do sometimes hang long on their hinges," notes Adams.

Hailing then went to a shop in Wolverhampton,

> the most abominable pi-receptacle one could imagine. There were neither quoins, furniture, leads, nor reglet, except a box full of broken pieces about the length of one's finger, and when a bill had to be set, the practice was for one to set the lines and another the reglets — the latter occupying the most time. There was, however, a mighty pyramid of pi and, like Aunt Chloe's big drawer, all the short sorts were there, you *only* had to find them! The old tale — the men had been on piece — no pay for "dis." Jobs dropped for sorts — picked — pi — pyramid.

MEMOIRS OF A SOCIAL ATOM

THE MACHINERY AND APPURTENANCES of the office were of a very primitive character compared with those of newspaper offices now. Down in the cellar (in one corner of which, by the way, was the only convenience in the establishment) was an old wooden press, and a cylinder machine that was turned by a handle. One man, with another to feed the machine and a boy to take off the printed sheets, could turn out the whole issue of the journal in an hour. The four pages of the paper were made up by old Mr. Hadley himself, who, when he ran short of matter or desired to curtail expenses, used to fill up a couple of columns of space with a huge standing advertisement of Grimstone's Eye Snuff — a patent commodity that has long since disappeared from the market. The formes were locked up with wooden quoins and sidesticks, and then carried below to the machine. One day a page was wrecked at the foot of the cellar stairs, whereupon a lad in the office pointed to the mass of pie and cried to the man who had been carrying the forme, "There it is, sir!" But I daresay it will require a printer to understand the ludicrous humour of the incident. Another feature of our working-day life that will be better understood by printers than by the public was the difficulty we experienced in working by candle-light. The candles were fixed in little leaden sconces, which were in their turn fixed in the "c" box of the case. When the candles guttered, as they did very often, for they were of the commonest quality, the box was filled with tallow and the air with imprecations. It will be seen from all this that our office was a very old-fashioned affair. We had old-fashioned ways, too, one of which was that of keeping a galley of standing headings for use when required. A revolution broke out in Paris in the second year of my apprenticeship. But there had been a revolution in Paris eighteen years before. And there in 1848, among the standing headings on the galley, was a line in big type that had done duty in 1830 — "The French Revolution."

❋❋❋

The tracts were of course explanatory of republican principles. Some I gave to school children to give to their teachers; some I hung on bushes by the highway; others I distributed among the inmates of the common lodging-houses at which I slept.

... Then I thought that my own people were at that very hour sauntering through pleasant lanes and pastures at home, while I, a solitary wanderer on the face of the earth, knew not a soul that I met. For a time I felt melancholy and depressed, and wished the long tramp was over.

Besides the bundle of tracts, I was not burdened with much baggage. A small parcel contained everything. Printers need to carry few tools. A composing stick and an apron were all I required to begin work anywhere, and even these were not indispensable. I called at all the newspaper offices on the route, begging some brother man to give me leave to toil. Not an odd job anywhere, nor any relief either except a shilling at Birmingham when I showed my indentures, for I was not a member of the union, there being then no branch at Cheltenham or Coniston. The times were out of joint. It was the winter of the Crimean War —the severest as regards weather, the dreariest as regards depression, the direst as regards distress, that we had had for years. I find in my old diary a note on the state of the country: — "Everywhere the cry is want of work."

✵✵✵

Mark Twain knew something of the tramp in America — especially the travelling "comp.," who "flitted by in the summer and tarried a day, with his wallet stuffed with one shirt and a hatful of handbills; for if he couldn't get any type to set, he would do a temperance lecture." I also knew the character, long before I became a tramp myself.

Some of the fraternity came once and were seen no more; others came round as often as the regulations of the trade society enabled them to draw relief. A man belonging to the former class — this was in 1848 — persuaded me to give him a shilling for writing an acrostic, and next night was seen gesticulating on a Chartist platform, partly for my edification. Two members of the latter class were rather famous in their day. One was the Bonny Light Horseman; another the Prince of Munster.

I had a pretty long acquaintance with the Prince of Munster. Dominic Macarthy had worked for a few months on *Galignani's Messenger* in Paris, and on the strength of this circumstance was considered a person of some note in the trade. He was a good workman; he possessed considerable intelligence; but he was afflicted with an incurable desire for roaming about the country whenever the proper season came round. Every year, or at least as often as relief could be obtained at the societies in the various towns through which he passed, the Prince was accustomed to make his appearance. It frequently happened that a job was to be had in the office in which I was apprenticed, and Dominic in this way became a familiar character in our establishment. As a lad, I liked nothing better than a crack with the royal "comp." Not that I think now that his habits or his influence were altogether wholesome for a youth of an impressionable temperament; for I recollect that he used, when he had the means, to bring into the office a supply of spirits to serve him till he could visit the public-house again. Now and then his royal highness would disappear beneath his "frame," and emerge from his seclusion wiping his mouth with the back of his hand, and discharging through the office an odour of Old Tom.

During the few days he remained at a time —and he never remained much longer than a week together — he had frequent "bouts." I remember that he defended these weaknesses of his on the ground that Buchan or some writer on hygienic matters contended that occasional excesses in intoxicating drinks had a healthy effect on the person who gave way to them. Dominic, as I have said, was never able to stay long in one place. When he got his wages, or as much of them as he had not anticipated, on a Saturday night, we could never be sure that he would turn in again on the Monday morning. Indeed, if he had nothing to draw, he was liable to disappear any day. When this happened, we would see nothing more of him till he came his rounds again a year later. The passion for roving was too strong to be resisted for many days together. The Prince could no more settle in one town in summer-time than a swallow can resist the impulse to seek another clime. Later on in life I made Dominic's acquaintance in London. There he invariably spent the winter months hanging about the office of the society in Racquet Court, and getting an occasional job as a "grass hand," until the return of spring enabled him to resume his vagabond life.

Some years passed. I was then in Newcastle. One night, when leaving the office, I heard my name pronounced as I passed a ragged figure standing near the door. Turning round, I discovered that I had been accosted by my old friend the Prince of Munster. His highness was raggeder, haggarder, and dirtier than I had ever seen him before. A quarter of a century of wandering hither and thither, together with the unknown quantity of spirits he must have consumed in that time, had told heavily on the Prince. I took him home with me; I gave him a good supper; I supplied him with a suit of old clothes; and I set him on his way rejoicing with a few shillings in his pocket. I never saw him again. The probability is that he died in some workhouse hospital or other.

Dominic Macarthy always seemed to me a type of the vagabond class. And I never think of him, and of my own feelings when I first made his acquaintance, without believing that I had a narrow escape of becoming a vagabond too.

A "TRAMP" PRINTING OFFICE.

A FLOATING JOB-PRINTING OFFICE on the Alabama River, well equipped and with a full stock of printing supplies, has come to light. The proprietor, his wife and five children occupy the front part of the craft, and the presses, chases and cases the rear. When the gang plank is hauled in it is understood that business is over for the day. It is said that the printer does a good business. Having no taxes or license to pay, and no house rent to bother him, he can do work cheaper than his competitors on land. His craft bears no name, and when last heard of was moored at the foot of Commerce street, Montgomery.

J. P. INGRAM:
AT THE CAPE.

HOW TYPE IS MEASURED IN THE DIAMOND FIELDS.

WHEN I ARRIVED AT KIMBERLY, after a year's service in a light cavalry regiment in Basutoland, I was pretty flush, having, about £50 or £60 in cash and a good horse, and consequently was in no hurry to look for work. After putting up my horse, and engaging a room at the hotel, I started out to have a "good time." As Kimberly, like most mining towns, is a lively sort of a place, it did not take long to run through my little sack. At the end of two weeks I found myself broke, or very nearly so, and thought it would be a good idea to go to the newspaper office and see if there was any chance to go to work.

When I entered the office — shanty would be a better name — of the *Diamond News*, I found it deserted, so I picked up a paper and sat down to wait till some one came in. Presently I heard a snore from behind the press, and upon investigation, I found a man stretched upon a pile of a paper fast asleep. I yelled at him and shook him, and finally succeeded in bringing him to his senses. He sat up, and after staring at me for a few minutes, asked me who I was and what the deuce I wanted.

I told him I was a printer, and wanted to go to work if possible.

"A printer! Well, I'll be d—d!" he exclaimed, and he slowly arose and steadying himself against the fly-wheel of the press, he stared at me as if I was some dime museum freak. "Why, where in the name of thunder did you come from?"

"From Basutoland," I answered. "I went to the front with the Kimberly Horse and put in a year killing Kafirs. And now, as I am pretty nearly broke, I suppose I shall have to go to work. So If you will tell me where I can find the foreman, I'll brace him."

"I'm the foreman, and by jingo, you've just struck the right shop. Printers are scarce in this part of the world, and those we have are seldom sober enough to work. The only man I could rely upon was arrested yesterday for illicit diamond buying. So if you want to go to work you can take his place and start in as soon as you please. I think Toby Butler is in the canteen on the corner. He generally hangs out there during the heat of the day and comes to work in the evening and early in the morning. You can't work in the middle of the day in this country; it's too hot. So let's go and I'll introduce you."

He took me into the saloon, where we found Toby seated at a table playing cards with the editor and a Boer farmer and drinking gin and lime-juice. The two time hands were taking a snooze on the veranda.

We went up to the bar, and after calling up the gang, and introducing me, the foreman set up the drinks and then asked Toby if it was not about time to go to work.

"Well, I'm just in the middle of a game," said Toby. "If you'll take my place, I'll start in now."

The foreman agreed to play his hand, and after taking another drink Toby and I returned to the office. I found a good long primer case and a bourgeois case about half full. The copy was kept in a cigar box, and we helped ourselves, of course picking out all the poetry and anything else that we considered phat.

As soon as it became dark, we lighted candles and stuck them around the cases. It took me some little time to get used to them. I would knock them down with my arm when reaching for the cap-case, or set my copy on fire, and every now and then a sudden gust of wind would blow them out, to say nothing of filling my case with candle grease. When I made a dig for a lowercase "d," I would lift about half a pound of them in a solid lump.

About 10 o'clock the foreman came in, pretty well loaded, and asked me how I was getting along.

I answered that I was doing as well as might be expected under the circumstances, as I had not set type for a couple of years, and I had never worked with a torchlight procession around my case before. I told him that I had run out of lowercase "d," and asked him where I should get some.

"Oh, use italic, or any type that will justify. Everything goes here. But it's time to knock off now, so let's go and have a nightcap."

We adjourned to the canteen and had several night-caps, and then after Toby and I had packed the foreman home and put him in his little bed, I thought it was about time to turn in myself.

The next morning they were all on deck at daylight. The two time hands looked rather seedy, but the foreman was as fresh as a lark. We worked until about ten in the morning, and then played cards, boozed and slept till about four o'clock in the afternoon, when those that were able went to work again till nine or ten o'clock at night.

On Saturday when I made out my bill, I asked Toby how much they paid per thousand.

"Oh, we don't get paid by the thousand. We get paid by the column. You see this stick? Well, it was originally the length of a column of the paper, but occasionally we whittle a piece off, and now it is about three inches short. We get fourteen shillings a column."

As that would be at the rate of $1.10 per thousand, I thought South Africa was a pretty good place for a printer. I had measured up my string and was about to turn it in, when Toby stopped me.

"Say, hold on a minute. You and I divide up the type the time hands set. We have to correct their dirty proofs, and so I think we are entitled to it."

I was perfectly satisfied to paste about four columns or more on my string, and suggested that we measure the ads the foreman set.

But Toby thought that would be going a little too far. The office might kick. But we might cut another inch off the measuring stick.

When I left Kimberly, six months later, that stick was about half its original size.

J. B. GRAHAM

JARED "JERRY" BENEDICT GRAHAM (1839–1929) apprenticed as devil on the Rochester, New York, *Advertiser*. He went to New York City and worked on the *Herald, Tribune* and *World*, "when those papers were presided over by the elder Bennett, Horace Greeley and Manton Marble." In 1860 he sailed to San Francisco via the Isthmus. Two years later he followed the silver trail to Virginia City, Nevada. Mark Twain and Dan de Quille were at that time local editors of the *Territorial Enterprise*. Graham returned to New York in 1865. He started papers in Michigan and Colorado, the latter purchased at $9,000, dwindled in four years with the failing claims; he left town with $15. He also worked in Wyoming before returning to New York and finally retiring, with "bad eyes and queer fingers," at 58.

His 1915 memoir, *Handset Reminiscences* is a rich tale of typographical tourism and recollections of the many colorful figures he knew. The strongest impressions were made by men of the New York *Herald* when Graham was a youngster — from the foreman, Smythe, who would drink and fight all night then sleep sitting in a chair for an hour before drinking a cup of coffee and returning to work, to "Jack Watson, whom we called 'Jack Falstaff,' for he took in hand every new 'Prince Hal' who came to the chapel and graduated him as a rounder; 'Old Fegee,' a reformed sailor, who was shipwrecked many times and for years marooned on a South Sea island"; to "Slug 11," an irritable drunk, who settled down during his periods of sobriety. Once he pretended to have lost an eye and presented to the Boston chapel a bloody codfish eyeball while his own eye was bandaged. By this ruse he raised $60: "I had plenty of eyes, except red eyes, so I transferred the appropriation to the department of ways and means; and was by this overt act ostracised from the city of beans and intellectuality."

THE FIRST SILVER BOOM

IF YOU WERE A POOR DEVIL of a typesticker — a Johnny-come-lately in one of the strangest of strange places — and you had just got in a night at $1 per thousand, and on the way to your room, on the main street, at considerable intervals you should stumble over three horrid cadavers, and the cheerful information had been imparted to you that you might expect a similar experience on the following night, and every other night, and that if a policeman were standing in a doorway close by he would merely shrug his shoulders when the several impediments turned up their toes, and in the morning would order a cart and have the remains, boots and all, dumped into a trench in the outskirts, thus closing the incidents; and that the policemen of the place were all instructed to not, under certain conditions, interfere with any amount of shooting, cutting, clubbing, or any other process of cadaver-making that might happen on the main street or any other street, would you have the nerve to continue on to your domicile, partake of a refreshing, dreamless sleep, and next day return to the office to get in "another one," or would you watch for the dawn, go paste your string, turn it over to the "Shylock" and incontinently hit the trail for other scenes?

This is not a hypothetical question — not a suppositious one at all events—for it brings up an incident just as it happened to me in the spring of 1862, a few days after my arrival in Virginia City, Nevada. There was a dearth of printers, and cases had been handed me by the benevolent and gentlemanly foreman of the Union; and it may be as well to say here that I held them down for two years, when I was fired for insubordination.

It was during the first silver boom. There were fifteen thousand people in the city—then but two years old as time is counted, but exceedingly old in iniquity. Everybody had money to burn, and it might as well have been burned for all the good the bulk of it did — squandered as fast as made. There were few homes. New comers and old were in luck to find clean rooms and a place where square meals were served. More than half of the population was made up of disreputables, including hundreds of desperadoes who had graduated in played-out gold camps of California and lived to get away. These were doing most of the shooting, and to save being bankrupted by court expenses the authorities allowed them to shoot without let or hindrance, so long as they did not molest or injure reputable citizens.

And say, maybe you think it wasn't a picnic for those unregenerate cut-throats. On one occasion the blood-letting was so frequent that the Union took on a moral spasm and scathingly denounced not only the bad men, but the authorities for permitting such goings on. That night a man of blood made a break to get back at the Union, and it happened that I had a close call. I have never had to put a peg there to remember it. My stand stood next to a front window. About the hour when graveyards yawn I was "pegging away," and just reaching for a capital C, when a bullet crashed through the glass, and passing close to my ear, sank into the capital B box.

The contents went swarming, like sure-enough bees. So did the printers in my alley, without waiting to be called out by the father of the chapel. After that I never worked in that window at night without a curtain between me and the street; and that was the only time that violence was offered me, albeit I was an eye-witness to many a shooting scrape and hundreds of bad men got their eternal deservings while I was in the city.

At this time Mark Twain (Sam Clemens) was a reporter on the *Territorial Enterprise,* and I presume incidentally gathering his notes for "Roughing It." He did not tell in his book of interesting happenings, humorous and otherwise, that would have filled the volumes of a small library. I have in mind one in particular that had Mark himself in the cast.

One day, with my sleeves rolled to the elbows, I was "throwing in" when a tall, gaunt, red-headed stranger came, with military tread, into the composing-room, and advancing several paces stood there as if transfixed. He had on a slouch hat, a travel-stained, old-fashioned linen duster, that reached to his heels, and in his hand was a large "carpet-bag," such as our fathers used to carry. Silently he surveyed the dozen or more printers, until his eyes rested on me. Then the bag dropped to the floor as if released by an automatic spring. With a movement like Hamlet's ghost he advanced to my side, seized my arm, stripped it to the shoulder, and tragically pointing to a vaccination scar, exclaimed:

"Behold, the mark! It is, it is my long lost brother. Found at last! Now may all the gods at once be praised. Friends, countrymen and brethren, you votaries of rotgut, let us all repair to the nearest inn and absorb, say, four fingers, by way of celebrating this glad reunion."

This was Artemus Ward (Charles F. Browne), with whom I had worked on the Cleveland *Plain Dealer* at the time he was its local editor and writing for its Saturday issues the sketches that made him famous. No one who had seen him once could ever forget him.

There was no work for me during his four days' stay. He had been announced by the papers to lecture that night, but not a bill had been posted.

"Brother," he said to me, "I must say unto all the people, yea, upon the walls of the city, I am come; lest peradventure, they know it not, and bring not their shekels unto my hopper. Now, therefore, prithee, go thou with me to spread the glad tidings, and verily when we have done this thing we will repair again to the wine cellar of the publican — which, I know by the cut of his jib he's a d——d sinner."

These were his exact words, as nearly as I can remember. So overflowing with humor was Charley Browne that he seldom uttered a sober sentence, and one of his favorite modes of expression was in imitation of Holy Writ.

I thought I was in for a regular billposting job, but submitted. We went to the *Enterprise* office, and procuring a sheet of 24 by 36 newsprint, with a blue pencil he wrote upon it this legend:

ARTEMUS WARD
WILL SPEAK HIS PIECE
HERE
TONIGHT.

This he tacked on the door of Maguire's opera house, and though the theatre was packed each night of his stay it was the only posting that was done.

I do not believe Mark Twain ever entertained an idea that he was to really write a book until that lecture gave him a jolt. Anyway, from that time there was a vein of wit all through his newspaper work that was not there before, and many of his brightest hits seemed to have a familiar cast to those who heard the lecture; though they were really original. He was following a new train of thought — evolving an idea — and I have since believed that, as a genius, he was dreaming until Artemus Ward awakened him to his capabilities; that no doubt the sayings of the greatest American wit preceding him had always been green in his memory.

A row of seats close to the stage at Maguire's, usually set apart for newspaper men, was called "the printers' pew." In one of those seats was Mark, with open mouth. I know, because I sat beside him. The lecture, announced as "Babes in the Wood," without reference to its title was a continuous string of grotesque and absurd witticisms — so keen, dry and far-fetched that for a moment no one could see a point, and each time a laugh was due the lecturer would pause until it came. With the first guffaw the audience seemed to catch on, and then it would go off like a corn-popper.

When the uproar had subsided, suddenly a spasmodic "Haw, haw, haw!" unreserved as if from a burro corral, would attract all eyes to the "pew," and at each interruption Artemus paused again, and glaring in mock anger, said something funny, like, "Has it been watered today?" once saying, "You must now all admit the truth of the old saw that 'he who laughs last laughs best.'"

Little did he think that that same laugh convulsed a greater genius than himself. Its tardiness was of a piece with Mark Twain's poky nature even to his deliberate, drawling way of speaking, so often mentioned as one of his characteristics.

During his brief stay in Virginia City Artemus had an elaborate introduction to its wild and woolly ways. He visited every place where there were "sights," everywhere accompanied by a crowd of convivial spirits who (while enjoying his genial humor) were not unmindful of his prodigal generosity.

Once as he was passing a gambling den two Philistines ran into the street and began shooting at each other. A dead man was the result. "Poor devil," said Artemus. "They told me over in San Francisco you people often get real mad, like that, but I was hoping my 'Babes' would make you more tractable and better natured. I see it's no use. Thinking of the place he's on his way to makes me thirst for ice water. Let us repair to the deadfall of the publican yet again."

Artemus went by stage from Nevada to the city of the Saints, where he hobnobbed with Brigham Young, whom he referred to in his book as "the much-married man." On his last night in Virginia City, after the lecture, he with a crowd visited a variety show, and to gratify his inordinate appetite for excitement and fun went on the stage as a blackface artist. Not even the actors knew who he was, & his friends and the manager never gave it away, for he was as bad an actor as he was great as a humorist.

TWAIN KNEW JOURNALISM from Alpha to Omaha. As a boy he had apprenticed on his brother Orion's paper in Hannibal, Missouri. His "Recollections of a Country Printing-Office" were delivered as a speech to the United Typothetæ of America. There, among friends, he recalled, "I can still see that printing-office of prehistoric times yet, with its horse bills on the wall; its 'd' boxes clogged with tallow, because we always stood the candle in the 'k' box at night; its towel, which was not considered soiled until it could stand alone, and other signs and symbols that marked the establishment of that kind in the Mississippi valley. I can see also the tramping journeyman, who fitted up in the summer and tarried a day, with his wallet stuffed with one shirt & a hatful of handbills; for if he couldn't get any type to set, he would do a temperance lecture. His way of life was simple, his needs not complex; all he wanted was plate and bed and money enough to get drunk on and he was satisfied."

Among his writings on journalism and country papers are "How I Edited an Agricultural Paper Once," which appeared in the *Galaxy*, vol. 10, July 1870, and the equally facetious "I Run for Governor." Both of these tales use hyperbole to great effect. In an 1872 speech on "The Sins of the Press," Twain expressed himself:

A Detroit paper once said that I was in the constant habit of beating my wife and that I still keep this recreation up although I had crippled her for life and she was no longer able to keep out of my way when I came home in my usual frantic frame of mind. Now scarcely the half of that was true.

Our story, "Journalism in Tennessee," first appeared in the *Buffalo Express*, September 4, 1869. Where the other two stories use Surreal exaggeration and absurdity to make their point, in this tale he uses violence. Revolvers were called the "great leveler" in the Old West, but Twain uses laughter as an equalizer. His humor frees his writing from both terror and the cloying piety that permeated late-Victorian thought and writing. This folk humor was classified by Mikhail Bakhtin as "grotesque realism." The essential principle of this is degradation of all that is lofty or spiritual to an earthy level. This "material bodily principle" has its roots in the Saturnalias of antiquity and was handed down from Petronius and Juvenal to Rabelais, Cervantes, Sterne and thence to later writers like Twain. The world turned inside-out creates a carnival atmosphere where everyone is laughed at: the mockers are also mocking themselves.

Twain believed in the power of the press for good, but also recognized it as a force of persuasion that could bend the truth: "Let sleeping dogs lie. Right. Still, when there is much at stake it is better to get a newspaper to do it!"

Journalism in Tennessee.

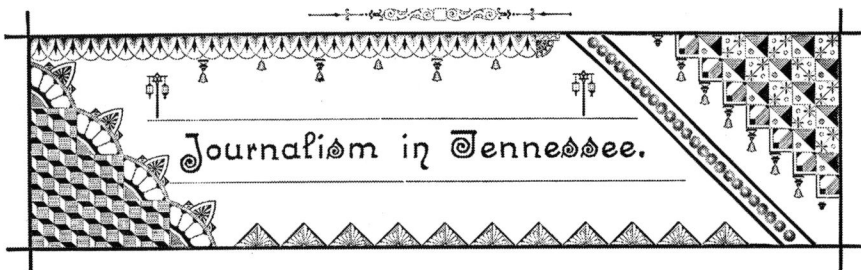

The editor of the Memphis *Avalanche* swoops thus mildly down upon a correspondent who posted him as a Radical:— "While he was writing the first word, the middle, dotting his i's, crossing his t's, and punching his period, he knew he was concocting a sentence that was saturated with infamy and reeking with falsehood."—*Exchange*.

I WAS TOLD BY THE PHYSICIAN that a Southern climate would improve my health, and so I went down to Tennessee, and got a berth on the *Morning Glory and Johnson County War-Whoop* as associate editor. When I went on duty I found the chief editor sitting tilted back in a three-legged chair with his feet on a pine table. There was another pine table in the room and another afflicted chair, and both were half buried under newspapers and scraps and sheets of manuscript. There was a wooden box of sand, sprinkled with cigar stubs and "old soldiers," and a stove with a door hanging by its upper hinge. The chief editor had a long-tailed black cloth frock-coat on, and white linen pants. His boots were small and neatly blacked. He wore a ruffled shirt, a large seal-ring, a standing collar of obsolete pattern, and a checkered neckerchief with the ends hanging down. Date of costume about 1848. He was smoking a cigar, and trying to think of a word, and in pawing his hair he had rumpled his locks a good deal. He was scowling fearfully, and I judged that he was concocting a particularly knotty editorial. He told me to take the exchanges and skim through them and write up the "Spirit of the Tennessee Press," condensing into the article all of their contents that seemed of interest.

I wrote as follows:

SPIRIT OF THE TENNESSEE PRESS

The editors of the *Semi-Weekly Earthquake* evidently labor under a misapprehension with regard to the Dallyhack railroad. It is not the object of the company to leave Buzzardville off to one side. On the contrary, they consider it one of the most important points along the line, and consequently can have no desire to slight it. The gentlemen of the *Earthquake* will, of course, take pleasure in making the correction.

John W. Blossom, Esq., the able editor of the *Higginsville Thunderbolt and Battle Cry of Freedom*, arrived in the city yesterday. He is stopping at the Van Buren House.

We observe that our contemporary of the *Mud Springs Morning Howl* has fallen into the error of supposing that the election of Van Werter is not an established fact, but he will have discovered his mistake before this reminder reaches him, no doubt. He was doubtless misled by incomplete election returns.

It is pleasant to note that the city of Blathersville is endeavoring to contract with some New York gentlemen to pave its well-nigh impassable streets with the Nicholson pavement. The *Daily Hurrah* urges the measure with ability, and seems confident of ultimate success.

I passed my manuscript over to the chief editor for acceptance, alteration, or destruction. He glanced at it and his face clouded. He ran his eye down the pages, and his countenance grew portentous. It was easy to see that something was wrong. Presently he sprang up and said:

"Thunder and lightning! Do you suppose I am going to speak of those cattle that way? Do you suppose my subscribers are going to stand such gruel as that? Give me the pen!"

I never saw a pen scrape and scratch its way so viciously, or plow through another man's verbs and adjectives so relentlessly. While he was in the midst of his work, somebody shot at him through the open window, and marred the symmetry of my ear.

"Ah," said he, "that is that scoundrel Smith, of the *Moral Volcano* — he was due yesterday." And he snatched a navy revolver from his belt and fired — Smith dropped, shot in the thigh. The shot spoiled Smith's aim, who was just taking a second chance and he crippled a stranger. It was me. Merely a finger shot off.

Then the chief editor went on with his erasure; and interlineations. Just as he finished them a hand grenade came down the stove-pipe, and the explosion shivered the stove into a thousand fragments. However, it did no further damage, except that a vagrant piece knocked a couple of my teeth out.

"That stove is utterly ruined," said the chief editor.

I said I believed it was.

"Well, no matter — don't want it this kind of weather. I know the man that did it. I'll get him. Now, here is the way this stuff ought to be written."

I took the manuscript. It was scarred with erasures and interlineations till its mother wouldn't have known it if it had had one. It now read as follows:

SPIRIT OF THE TENNESSEE PRESS

The inveterate liars of the *Semi-Weekly Earthquake* are evidently endeavoring to palm off upon a noble and chivalrous people another of their vile and brutal falsehoods with regard to that most glorious conception of the nineteenth century, the Ballyhack railroad. The idea that Buzzardville was to be left off at one side originated in their own fulsome brains — or rather in the settlings which they regard as brains. They had better swallow this lie if they want to save their abandoned reptile carcasses the cowhiding they so richly deserve.

That ass, Blossom, of the *Higginsville Thunderbolt and Battle Cry of Freedom*, is down here again sponging at the Van Buren.

We observe that the besotted blackguard of the *Mud Springs Morning Howl* is giving out, with his usual propensity for lying, that Van Werter is not elected. The heaven-born mission of journalism is to disseminate truth; to eradicate error; to educate, refine, and elevate the tone of public morals and manners, and make all men more gentle, more virtuous, more charitable, and in all ways better, and holier, and happier; and yet this blackhearted scoundrel degrades his great office persistently to the dissemination of falsehood, calumny, vituperation, and vulgarity.

Blathersville wants a Nicholson pavement — it wants a jail and a poorhouse more. The idea of a pavement in a one-horse town composed of two gin-mills, a blacksmith shop, and that mustard-plaster of a newspaper, the *Daily Hurrah*! The crawling insect, Buckner, who edits the *Hurrah*, is braying about his business with his customary imbecility, and imagining that he is talking sense.

"Now that is the way to write — peppery and to the point. Mush-and-milk journalism gives me the fan-tods."

About this time a brick came through the window with a splintering crash, and gave me a considerable of a jolt in the back. I moved out of range — I began to feel in the way.

The chief said, "That was the Colonel, likely. I've been expecting him for two days. He will be up now right away."

He was correct. The Colonel appeared in the door a moment afterward with a dragoon revolver in his hand.

He said, "Sir, have I the honor of addressing the poltroon who edits this mangy sheet?"

"You have. Be seated, sir. Be careful of the chair, one of its legs is gone. I believe I have the honor of addressing the putrid liar, Colonel Blatherskite Tecumseh?"

"Right, Sir. I have a little account to settle with you. If you are at leisure we will begin."

"I have an article on the 'Encouraging Progress of Moral and Intellectual Development in America' to finish, but there is no hurry. Begin."

Both pistols rang out their fierce clamor at the same instant. The chief lost a lock of his hair, and the Colonel's bullet ended its career in the fleshy part of my thigh. The Colonel's left shoulder was clipped a little. They fired again. Both missed their men this time, but I got my share, a shot in the arm. At the third fire both gentlemen were wounded slightly, and I had a knuckle chipped. I then said, I believed I would go out and take a walk, as this was a private matter, and I had a delicacy about participating in it further. But both gentlemen begged me to keep my seat, and assured me that I was not in the way.

They then talked about the elections and the crops while they reloaded, and I fell to tying up my wounds. But presently they opened fire again with animation, and every shot took effect — but it is proper to remark that five out of the six fell to my share. The sixth one mortally wounded the Colonel, who remarked, with fine humor, that he would have to say good morning now, as he had business uptown. He then inquired the way to the undertaker's and left.

The chief turned to me and said, "I am expecting company to dinner, and shall have to get ready. It will be a favor to me if you will read proof and attend to the customers."

I winced a little at the idea of attending to the customers, but I was too bewildered by the fusillade that was still ringing in my ears to think of anything to say.

He continued, "Jones will be here at three — cowhide him. Gillespie will call earlier, perhaps — throw him out of the window. Ferguson will be along about four — kill him. That is all for today, I believe. If you have any odd time, you may write a blistering article on the police — give the chief inspector rats. The cowhides are under the table; weapons in the drawer — ammunition there in the corner — lint and bandages up there in the pigeonholes. In case of accident, go to Lancet, the surgeon, downstairs. He advertises — we take it out in trade."

He was gone. I shuddered. At the end of the next three hours I had been through perils so awful that all peace of mind and all cheerfulness were gone from me. Gillespie had called and thrown me out of the window. Jones arrived promptly, and when I got ready to do the cowhiding he took the job off my hands. In an encounter with a stranger, not in the bill of fare, I had lost my scalp. Another stranger, by the name of Thompson, left me a mere wreck and ruin of chaotic rags. And at last, at bay in the corner, and beset by an infuriated mob of editors, blacklegs, politicians, and desperadoes, who raved and swore and flourished their weapons about my head till the air shimmered with glancing flashes of steel, I was in the act of resigning my berth on the paper when the chief arrived, and with him a rabble of charmed and enthusiastic friends. Then ensued a scene of riot and carnage such as no human pen, or steel one either, could describe. People were shot, probed, dismembered, blown up, thrown out of the window. There was a brief tornado of murky blasphemy, with a confused and frantic war-dance glimmering through it, and then all was over. In five minutes there was silence, and the gory chief and I sat alone and surveyed the sanguinary ruin that strewed the floor around us.

He said, "You'll like this place when you get used to it."

I said, "I'll have to get you to excuse me; I think maybe I might write to suit you after a while; as soon as I had had some practice and learned the language I am confident I could. But, to speak the plain truth, that sort of energy of expression has its inconveniences, and a man is liable to interruption.

"You see that yourself. Vigorous writing is calculated to elevate the public, no doubt, but then I do not like to attract so much attention as it calls forth. I can't write with comfort when I am interrupted so much as I have been to-day. I like this berth well enough, but I don't like to be left here to wait on the customers. The experiences are novel, I grant you, and entertaining, too, after a fashion, but they are not judiciously distributed. A gentleman shoots at you through the window and cripples me; a bombshell comes down the stovepipe for your gratification and sends the stove door down my throat; a friend drops in to swap compliments with you, and freckles me with bullet-holes till my skin won't hold my principles; you go to dinner, and Jones comes with his cowhide, Gillespie throws me out of the window, Thompson tears all my clothes off, and an entire stranger takes my scalp with the easy freedom of an old acquaintance; and in less than five minutes all the blackguards in the country arrive in their war-paint, and proceed to scare the rest of me to death with their tomahawks. Take it altogether, I never had such a spirited time in all my life as I have had to-day. No; I like you, and I like your calm unruffled way of explaining things to the customers, but you see I am not used to it. The Southern heart is too impulsive; Southern hospitality is too lavish with the stranger. The paragraphs which I have written to-day, and into whose cold sentences your masterly hand has infused the fervent spirit of Tennesseean journalism, will wake up another nest of hornets. All that mob of editors will come — and they will come hungry, too, and want somebody for breakfast. I shall have to bid you adieu. I decline to be present at these festivities. I came South for my health, I will go back on the same errand, and suddenly. Tennesseean journalism is too stirring for me."

After which we parted with mutual regret, and I took apartments at the hospital.

Women in the Printing Office.

THE NEW WOMAN has come to stay — in the factory, in the business office, and in the printing office. It matters not that she has been opposed here and there by trades unions and heads of families who wanted the work for themselves. The new woman came, saw, and conquered. The question is, are we better or worse off as a general result? Have women tended to reduce wages or to raise them? Have they exerted a refining influence in the offices where they are employed? We would be glad to say "yes" to all these questions, but incline to the opinion that while women have raised the standard of refinement in the printing office they have also tended to the reduction of wages, a reduction which has not even benefited the proprietors, but has been given to the public as a gratuity. Where a considerable number of men in a community decline to marry, or, what is the same in result, where a considerable number of women prefer to remain single, it follows that many of the single women must earn a livelihood outside of the home. Typesetting is an employment to which they are well fitted, and many of them gravitate to it. Sometimes they have worked into the places of heads of families, which is to be deplored, but cannot be helped. That their influence in the office is usually for good, there can be no doubt. Men grow gross when they herd too much by themselves, and the restraining presence of a bright girl in a composing room has put a stop to much profanity and ill talk. It has also influenced proprietors, in many cases, to make the composing rooms more cleanly and attractive, rendering them more like offices and less like workshops. To those men who object to woman in the printing office our advice is: Select a pretty, modest and amiable compositress, and take her out of the printing office by marrying her. If you cannot do this, because you already have a wife, encourage others to do it.

The Female Compositor

OF ALL THE OCCUPATIONS in which a woman can engage for the purpose of making a living the most thankless is that of setting type, says *The Denver Tribune*. The female compositor leads a weary and dreary life. She is never permitted to strike a fat take, she is denied the inestimable boon of setting up the thoughtful matter which emanates from the editorial room; she is never reckoned capable of handling manuscript, and the very idea of her being competent to set up a display head is deemed atrocious. She is expected to hammer away at miscellaneous reprint; the only bonanza she ever strikes is solid minion with an occasional oasis of leaded brevier when the business manager concludes that advertising is dull enough to admit of the biggest kind of type. But this is not all — no, the worst remains to be told. When the work is done for the day, it is not with the female printer as with others of the trade. She can not adjourn to a convenient and comfortable saloon and play pedro or old sledge for the beer or throw dice for five-cent cigars or jeff* for the drinks. She must pick her way home through all sorts of weather to a dreary room and cold bed. She has no wife to thrash, no children to scold, no furniture to break — none of those sweet luxuries which are supposed to be part and parcel of the glorious art preservative. As a class, female printers are diligent and worthy. They never "sojer," they never bother the editors for chewing tobacco; they never prowl around among

* Jeff = a game like dice, using blank spacing material and counting how many nicks fall upwards.

the exchanges for the *Police Gazette*; they never get themselves full of budge and try to clean out rival print shops; they never swear about the business manager; they do not smoke nasty old clay pipes, they never strike for more pay, they do not allude to editorial matter as "slush" or "frogwash;" in short, they are patient, gentle, conscientious and reliable. They peg right along for $7 a week, dress tidily, keep solid with the foreman, and, last of all, when the female compositor gets tired of her treadmill, unceasing round of toils, she marries the best looking printer in the shop, and then she becomes a verier slave than before.

Ye Ancient Typo

A Typographical Tourist of a Bygone Age

HE CAME IN YESTERDAY EVENING, and as he meandered around to a chair, he said he was a-weary and would rest.

His hair was as white as the driven snow; he could see with but one eye, over which was a glass — the other eye was sightless and didn't require any, so the iron frame of his spectacle had been relieved of the superfluous weight.

Then he asked how work was, for he was a printer of high degree, and for 59 years had he toiled at the "art preservative."

So he is at work to-day, this old man is. And as we look at him bending over his case, with the weight of 73 years upon his shoulders, it is hard to realize that he is not some untroubled spirit that has crawled out of an unquiet grave to "revisit the glimpses of the moon."

The *Jefferson City Tribune* says of him:

Tuesday morning George W. Matchett, a weather-beaten and venerable old man, stepped into our office and asked for work. He stated that he had walked all the way from Peoria, Illinois, was out of money, and unable to proceed any further on his way without assistance; that for many days he had subsisted on the charity of individuals by the way; his nights had been spent in barns and outhouses, and frequently with no other covering but the canopy of heaven. He was given "cases" and immediately began work. His history is, indeed, an eventful one, not devoid of romance. Born in Richmond, Va., in 1805, he is now 73 years of age; in 1819 he commenced his apprenticeship with his uncle, Richard Matchett, publisher of the Baltimore *Society Herald*. The *Herald* was worked on a Ramage press, made entirely of wood, except the bed, which was of stone; the platen was of mahogany; instead of rollers, balls were used, made of poplar, in the shape of a wooden bowl, with one handle; the inside of the bowl was filled with wool compactly pressed together, and covered with buckskin. What wonderful changes has he seen in fifty-nine years' labor in printing offices. After learning his trade he worked for Harper Brothers in New York in 1831; in 1832 he worked for Horace Greeley, on his paper called the *New Yorker*; in 1848 he worked in the *Republican* office, St. Louis; since that time he has visited and worked in every State in the Union, except Oregon. In 1837 he was engaged to be married to Miss Minerva Scott; the day appointed for the wedding, the clergymen and friends had assembled; while the expectant company were awaiting the entrance of the bride from an adjoining room, a shriek was heard, which startled all. The bride, decked with orange blossoms, had been stricken with heart disease, and before the hour arrived for the nuptial ceremonies, was cold in death. The remembrance of that sad event has haunted the old man ever since; he never married and from that fatal hour has been a wanderer, seeking in vain for rest. He started yesterday for Rice county, Kansas, where he expects to meet several friends of his early youth.

2 p.m. — The old man has just come from dinner. He has struck several "bowls," and after bidding the *Bazoo* an affectionate adieu, he "lit out" toward the sunset route.

THREE TOURISTS.

AMONG THE MANY typographical tourists who have arrived in Wichita lately are A. C. Emerick and S. D. Gates, who deposited traveling cards with the secretary of Wichita union yesterday, and whose appearance would attract attention almost anywhere. Mr. Emerick "sticks type" from a height of 6 feet 6 inches, while his partner, Mr. Gates, reaches up from a bare 5 feet. Notwithstanding his great length Mr. Emerick has but very little advantage in weight over his traveling companion, who makes up in width what he lacks in height. The gentlemen left New York city together and are now on a tour of the country. Mr. Emerick is the tallest printer in the country.

Another member of the craft who showed up at the *Eagle* office yesterday is Thomas McKenna. He is reputed to be one of the oldest printers in the country. He was old when the oldest printers on the *Eagle* were kids, and there is a legend about him to the effect that he was seen around the office when Gutenberg and Faust were making their first experiments with the movable types.

PERSONAL

Items Gleaned in the Hotel Corridors and from Various Other Sources.

"ART PRESERVATIVE," a typographical tourist hailing from a city famous for its salt baths, who has been snuffing dust in the Alamo city for the past week, has folded his tent and, like the Arab, silently stolen away—and the Mascottes bemoan the absence of the Chief Whangdoodle of the Flowery Kingdom.

The Greatest of Tramp Printers.

JOHN G. GANTT, the celebrated tramp printer, has been in this city during the past three days, says a Columbus special to the *Indianapolis Journal*. This remarkable man, who is known in almost every printing establishment in the central and southern states, is seventy years of age and has been constantly on the tramp since the close of the civil war. The longest tramp he ever made was in 1884, when he left this city and traveled through all of the states between here and Florida, and returned by the same route, reaching Cassopolis, Mich., just six months from the time he left here. He kept a careful record of the number of miles walked and the entire length of the journey was 2,800 miles. For a man then sixty-five years of age this certainly was a remarkable feat. This veteran printer has a great failing for drink, but his constant indulgence does not seem to have weakened his mental faculties, and he possesses a remarkable fund of information, picked up by reading and experience. He recently started a very unique newspaper called *Gantt's Typographical Tourist*. It is published "on the road," and gives interesting items concerning the craft.

BRET HARTE

Bret Harte admits that he learned the printer's trade. He says he could work six quarts of type per day on a hand press, and could correct a roller as good as anybody. — *Detroit Free Press*, 1876

BRET HARTE (1836–1902) was born in Albany, New York of Dutch and English ancestry. He was a published poet by the age of 11. He took a ship to San Francisco which was ship-wrecked. He worked as a miner, private tutor, shotgun rider on a stage coach and as a compositor on the *Golden Era* and the *Northern Californian* which published many of his short stories, leading to national fame. He satirized the white man's treatment of Indians, Chinese and Mexicans. When he described the massacre of Indians by whites in Eureka, California, he was fired from the *Northern Californian*. He described the California Gold Rush as a "Crusade without a cross, an exodus without a prophet." He was founding editor of the *Overland Monthly* at a fabulous salary. He was appointed U.S. Consul to Crefelt, Prussia in 1878, to replace Bayard Taylor who had died there. (Taylor, another printer, had tramped around Europe as a lad, and wrote volumes of travel books before becoming editor of the New York *Tribune*.) Harte was unhappy in Prussia and transferred to Glasgow, Scotland where he had an affair with another diplomat's wife. In 1885 he retired to London.

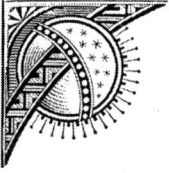

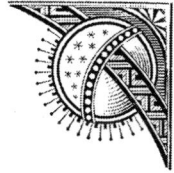

Wanted— A Printer.

"WANTED — A PRINTER," says a contemporary. Wanted, a mechanical curiosity, with brain and fingers — a thing that will set so many type in a day — a machine that will think and act, but still a machine — a being who undertakes the most systematic and monotonous drudgery, yet one the ingenuity of man has never supplanted mechanically — that's a printer.

A printer — yet for all his sometimes dissipated and reckless habits—a worker. At all times and hours, day and night; sitting up in a close, unhealthy office, when gay crowds are hurrying to the theatre—later still, when the street revelers are gone and the city sleeps—in the fresh air of the morning—in the broad and gushing sunlight—some printing machine is at the case, with its eternal unvarying *click! click!*

Click! click! the polished type fall into the stick; the mute integers of expression are marshaled into line, and march forth as immortal print. *Click!* and the latest intelligence becomes old—the thought a principle—the simple idea a living sentiment. *Click! click!* from grave to gay, item after item — a robbery, a murder, a bit of scandal, a graceful, a glowing thought — are in turn clothed by the impassive fingers of the machine, and set adrift in the sea of thought. He must not think of the future, nor recall the past—must not think of home, of kindred, of wife or of babe — his work lies before him, and thought is chained to his copy.

Ye who know him by his works, who read the papers and are quick at typographical errors — whose eye may rest on these mute evidences of ceaseless toil: correspondents, editors, and authors, who scorn the simple medium of your fame, think not that the printer is altogether a machine—think not that he is indifferent to the gem to which he is but the setter—but think a subtle ray may penetrate the recesses of his brain, or the flowers that he gathers may not leave some of their fragrance on his toil-worn fingers.

BILL NYE

EDGAR "BILL" NYE (1850–96), born in Maine, moved to Laramie, Wyoming, where he became judge, postmaster & founder of the *Laramie Boomerang* (which he named after his mule). In 1886, Joseph Pulitzer hired him on to the *New York World*, where he gained fame for his witty writing. Hicks remembered Pulitzer from the Saint Louis *Post-Dispatch*:

> Pulitzer rode to work every morning in a brougham drawn by a big iron-gray horse driven by a Negro. He wrote all the editorials for the paper and when he appeared at eight-thirty he would have the lead editorials for the day in his pocket, ready for the printers. Then he would disappear into his sanctum, a curtained alcove just off the city room. At ten o'clock he would be given the first corrected proof of his editorial, when he would go to work in earnest, making revision after revision, until Jack Williams, foreman of the composing room, would beg for a final O.K. so the paper could go to press. About noon he would go into the nearby saloon of Anthony & Kuhn, on Broadway, for a sandwich and a glass of beer. Late at night he would be in his den, writing editorials by the single gas jet, something that might have been a factor in his later blindness.

Nye's humorous columns were collected into books. He adopted the name "Bill Nye" after the card shark in Bret Harte's poem, "Plain Language from Truthful James." Nye and Will Visscher became friends while sojourning on newspapers in Cheyenne, Wyoming. Late in his career, Nye was associated with James Whitcomb Riley with whom he wrote two books. They also appeared together on the lecture circuit. He also traveled and lectured with Luther Burbank. Like Visscher and Twain he was quick to make fun of the "patron saint" of American printers, Benjamin Franklin.

B. FRANKLIN, DECEASED

BENJAMIN FRANKLIN, formerly of Boston, came very near being an only child. If seventeen children had not come to bless the home of Benjamin's parents, they would have been childless. Think of getting up in the morning and picking out your shoes and stockings from among seventeen pairs of them. Imagine yourself a child, gentle reader, in a family where you would be called upon, every morning, to select your own cud of spruce gum from a collection of seventeen similar cuds stuck on a window sill. And yet B. Franklin never murmured or repined. He desired to go to sea, and to avoid this he was apprenticed to his brother James, who was a printer. It is said that Franklin at once took hold of the great Archimedean lever, and jerked it early and late in the interests of freedom. It is claimed that Franklin at this time invented the deadly weapon known as the printer's towel. He found that a common crash towel could be saturated with glue, molasses, antimony, concentrated lye, and roller composition, and that after a few years of time and perspiration it would harden so that the "Constant Reader" or "Veritas" could be stabbed with it and die soon.

Many believe that Franklin's other scientific experiments were productive of more lasting benefit to mankind than this, but I do not agree with them.

This paper was called the *New England Courant*. It was edited jointly by James and Benjamin Franklin, and was started to supply a long-felt want. Benjamin edited a part of the time and James a part of the time. The idea of having two editors was not for the purpose of giving volume to the editorial page, but it was necessary for one to run the paper while the other was in jail. In those days you couldn't sass the king, and then, when the king came in the office the next day and stopped his paper, and took out his ad., you couldn't put it off on "our informant" and go right along with the paper. You had to go to jail, while your subscribers wondered why their paper did not come, and the paste soured in the tin dippers in the sanctum, and the circus passed by on the other side.

How many of us to-day, fellow journalists, would be willing to stay in jail while the lawn festival and the kangaroo came and went? Who, of all our company, would go to a prison cell for the cause of freedom while a double-column ad. of sixteen aggregated circuses, and eleven congresses of ferocious beasts, fierce and fragrant from their native lair, went by us?

At the age of 17, Ben got disgusted with his brother, and went to Philadelphia and New York, where he got a chance to "sub" for a few weeks, and then got a regular "sit." Franklin was a good printer, and finally got to be a foreman. He made an excellent foreman, sitting by the hour in the composing room and spitting on the stone, while he cussed the make-up and press work of the other papers. Then he would go into the editorial rooms and scare the editors to death with a wild shriek for more copy. He knew just how to conduct himself as a foreman, so that strangers would think he owned the paper.

In 1730, at the age of 24, Franklin married and established the *Pennsylvania Gazette*. He was then regarded as a great man, and most everyone took his paper. Franklin grew to be a great journalist, and spelled hard words with great fluency. He never tried to be a humorist in any of his newspaper work, and everybody respected him.

Along about 1746 he began to study the construction and habits of lightning, and inserted a local in his paper, in which he said that he would be obliged to any of his readers who might notice any new or odd specimens of lightning, if they would send them into the *Gazette* office by express for examination. Every time there was a thunder storm, Franklin would tell the foreman to edit the paper, and, armed with a string and an old fruit jar, he would go out on the hills and get enough lightning for a mess.

In 1753 Franklin was made postmaster-general of the colonies. He made a good postmaster-general, and people say there were less mistakes in distributing their mail than there has ever been since. If a man mailed a letter in those days, old Ben Franklin saw that it went where it was addressed.

Franklin frequently went over to England in those days, partly on business, and partly to shock the king. He used to delight in going to the castle with his breeches tucked in his boots, figuratively speaking, and attract a good deal of attention. It looked odd to the English, of course, to see him come into the royal presence, and, leaving his wet umbrella up against the throne, ask the king: "How's trade?" Franklin never put on any frills, but he was not afraid of a crowned head. He used to say, frequently, that to him a king was no more than a seven spot.

He did his best to prevent the Revolutionary war, but he couldn't do it. Patrick Henry had said that the war was inevitable, and given it permission to come, and it came. He also went to Paris and got acquainted with a few crowned heads there. They thought a good deal of him in Paris, and offered him a corner lot if he would build there and start a paper. They also promised him the county printing, but he said no, he would have to go back to America, or his wife might get uneasy about him.

Franklin wrote "Poor Richard's Almanac" in 1732–57, and it was republished in England. Benjamin Franklin had but one son, and his name was William. William was an illegitimate son, and, though he lived to be quite an old man, he never got over it entirely, but continued to be but an illegitimate son all his life. Everybody urged him to do differently, but he steadily refused to do so.

Knights of the Pen

WHEN YOU COME to think of it, it is surprising that so many newspaper men write so that any one but an expert can read it. The rapid and voluminous work, especially of daily journalism, knocks the beautiful business college penman, as a rule, higher than a kite. I still have specimens of my own handwriting that a total stranger could read.

I do not remember a newspaper acquaintance whose penmanship is so characteristic of the exacting neatness and sharp, clear cut style of the man, as is that of Eugene Field, of the *Chicago News*. As the "Nonpareil Writer" of the *Denver Tribune*, it was a mystery to me when he did the work which the paper showed each day as his own. You would sometimes find him at his desk, writing on large sheets of "print paper" with a pen and violet ink, in a hand that was as delicate as the steel plate of a bank note and the kind of work that printers would skirmish for. He would ask you to sit down in the chair opposite his desk, which had two or three old exchanges thrown on it. He would probably say, "Never mind those papers. I've read them. Just sit down on them if you want to." Encouraged by his hearty manner, you would sit down, and you would continue to sit down till you had protruded about three-fourths of your system through that hollow mockery of a chair. Then he would run to help you out and curse the chair, and feel pained because he had erroneously given you the ruin with no seat to it. He always felt pained over such things. He always suffered keenly and felt shocked over the accident until you had gone away, and then he would sigh heavily and "set" the chair again.

Frank Pixley, the editor of the *San Francisco Argonaut*, is not beautiful, though the *Argonaut* is. He is grim and rather on the Moses Montefiore style of countenance, but his hand-writing does not convey the idea of the man personally, or his style of dealing with the Chinese question. It is rather young looking, and has the uncertain manner of an eighteen-year-old boy.

Robert J. Burdette writes a small but plain hand, though he sometimes suffers from the savage typographical error that steals forth at such a moment as ye think not, and disfigures and tears and mangles the bright eyed children of the brain.

Very often we read a man's work and imagine we shall find him like it, cheery, bright and entertaining; but we know him and find that personally he is a refrigerator, or an egotist, or a man with a torpid liver and a nose like a rose geranium. You will not be disappointed in Bob Burdette, however — you think you will like him, and you always do. He will never be too famous to be a gentleman.

George W. Peck's hand is of the free and independent order of chirography. It is easy and natural, but not handsome. He writes very voluminously, doing his editorial writing in two days of the week, generally Friday and Saturday. Then he takes a rapid horse, a zealous bird dog and an improved double barrel duck destroyer and communes with nature.

Sam Davis, an old time Californian, and now in Nevada, writes the freest of any penman I know. When he is deliberate, he may be betrayed into making a deformed letter and a crooked mark attached to it, which he characterizes as a word. He puts a lot of these together and actually pays postage on the collection under the delusion that it is a letter, that it will reach its destination, and that it will accomplish its object.

He makes up for his bad writing, however, by being an unpublished volume of old time anecdotes and funny experiences.

Goodwin, of the old *Territorial Enterprise*, and Mark Twain's old employer, writes with a pencil in a methodical manner and very plainly. The way he sharpens a "hard medium" lead pencil and skins the apostle of the so-called Church of Jesus Christ of Latter Day Saints, makes my heart glad. Hardly a day passes that his life is not threatened by the low browed thumpers of Mormondom, and yet the old war horse raises the standard of monogamy and under the motto, "One country, one flag and one wife at a time," he smokes his old meerschaum pipe and writes a column of razor blades every day. He is the buzz saw upon which polygamy has tried to sit. Fighting these rotten institutions hand to hand and fighting a religious eccentricity through an annual message, or a feeble act of congress, are two separate and distinct things.

If I had a little more confidence in my longevity than I now have, I would go down there to the Valley of the Jordan, and I would gird up my loins, and I would write with that lonely warrior at Salt Lake, and with the aid and encouragement of our brethren of the press who do not favor the right of one man to marry an old woman's home, we would rotten egg the bogus Temple of Zion till the civilized world, with a patent clothes pin on its nose, would come and see what was the matter.

I see that my zeal has led me away from my original subject, but I haven't time to regret it now.

A PEACEABLE MAN

WILL L. VISSCHER always made a specialty of being a peaceable man. He would make most any sacrifice in order to secure general amnesty. I've known him to go around six blocks out of his way, to avoid a stormy interview with a belligerent dog. He was always very tender-hearted about dogs, especially the open-faced bulldog.

But he had a queer experience years ago, in St. Jo, Missouri. He had been city editor of the *Kansas City Journal* for some time, but one evening, while in the composing-room, the foreman told him that the place for the city editor was down stairs, in his office. He therefore ordered Visscher to go down there. Visscher said he would do so later on, after he got fatigued with the composing-room and wanted change of scene.

The foreman thereupon jumped on Mr. Visscher with a small pica wrought iron side stick. Visscher allowed that he was a peaceable man, but entered into the general chaos of double-leaded editorial, and hair and brass dashes, and dashes for liberty and heterogeneous "pi," and foot-sticks and teeth, with great zeal. He succeeded in putting a large doric head on the foreman, and although he was a peaceable man, he went down to the office and got his discharge for disturbing the discipline of the office.

He went to St. Jo the same day, and celebrated his debut into the town by a little game of what is known as "draw." He was fortunate in "filling his hand," and while he was taking in the stakes, a young man from Arkansas, who was in the game, nipped a two-dollar note in a quiet kind of way, which, however, was detected by Mr. V., who mentioned the matter at the time. This maddened the Arkansas man, and later on he put one of his long arms around Mr. Visscher so as to pinion him, and then smote him across the brow with an instrument, known to science as "the brass knucks." This irritated Mr. Visscher, and as soon as he had returned to consciousness he remarked that, although it was rather an up-hill job in Missouri, he was trying to be a peaceable man. He then broke the leg of a card-table over the head of the Arkansas man, and went to the doctor to get his own brow sewed on again.

While he was sitting in the doctor's office a friend of the Arkansas man came in and asked him to please stand up while he knocked him down. Visscher opened a little dialogue with the man, and drew him into conversation till he could open a case of surgical instruments near by, then he took out one of those knives that the surgeons use in removing the viscera from the leading gentleman at a post mortem.

"Now," said he, sharpening the knife on the stove-pipe and handing down a jar containing alcohol with a tumor in it, "I am a peaceful man and don't want any fuss; but if you insist on a personal encounter, I will slice off fragments of your physiognomy at my leisure, and for twenty minutes I will fill this office with your favorite features. I make a specialty of being a peaceable man, remember; but if you'll just say the word, I'll put overcoat button-holes and eyelet-holes and crazy-quilts all over your system. If I've got to kill off the poker-players of St. Jo before I can have any fun, I guess I might as well begin on you as on any one I know."

He then made a stab at the man and pinned his coat-tail to the door-frame. Fear loaned the bad man strength, and, splitting the coat-tail, he fled, taking little mementoes of the tumor-jar and shedding them in his flight. When Mr. Visscher went up to the *Herald* office soon after to get a job, he was introduced casually to the foreman, who said:

"Ah, this is the young man who licks the foreman of the paper he works on, is it? I am glad to meet you, Mr. Visscher. I am looking for a white-eyed son of a sea-cook who goes around over Missouri thumping the foremen of our leading journals. Come out into the ante-room, Mr. Visscher, till I jar your back teeth loose and send you to the morgue in a gunny-sack." Mr. Visscher repeated that he was trying to live in Missouri and be a peaceable man, but that if there was anything that he could do to make it pleasant for the foreman, he would cheerfully do it.

Mr. Visscher was a small man, but when he felt aggrieved about anything he was very harassing to his adversary. They "clinched" and threw each other back and forth across the hall with great vigor. When they stopped for breath, the foreman's coat was pulled over his head and the bosom of Mr. Visscher's shirt was hanging on the gas-jet. There were also two front teeth on the floor unaccounted for.

Visscher pinned on his shirt-bosom and said he was a peaceable man, but if the custom seemed to demand four fights in one day, he would try to conform to any local usage of the city. Wherever he went, he wanted to fall right into line and be one of the party.

When he got well he was employed on the *Herald*, and for four years edited the amnesty column of the paper successfully.

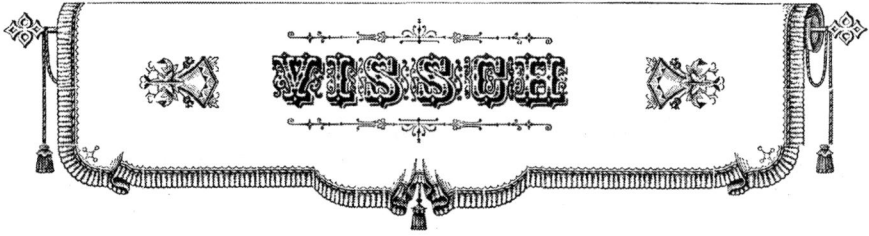

COLONEL WILL L. VISSCHER (1842–1924), born in Kentucky, wrote poems in Southern dialect and served with the 24th Kentucky Infantry on the Union side during the Civil War. (He was a hospital orderly during the war, but any veteran from Kentucky took the honorific title "Colonel.") After service in the army he received a degree in law from the University of Louisville in 1867, but "in spite of the fact that I received a law degree, I have never been in court except to plead guilty." He worked on the *Louisville Journal* as a paragrapher: an extra-editorial writer whose job was to create a witty apothegm or reflection on politics or the human condition in one brief paragraph. When it was absorbed by the *Courier* he began publishing a daily paper on a steamer plying between Louisville and New Orleans. Then began 30 years of wandering the country as a tramping printer and editor. He worked on papers in Kansas, Saint Joseph, Denver and the San Francisco Bay Area. After five years working on the press in San Francisco and Oakland, he hit the road as a comedian for three years with Captain Jack Crawford, an emulator of Buffalo Bill. The highlight of their tour was an attempt to stage an anti-Mormon play in Salt Lake City. They ended up in Chicago where Vissch returned to the press. Then he had a brief spell in Denver where his good friend Eugene Field edited the *Tribune*. The most famous fruit of Field and Vissch's friendship was Field's "Ballad of Slug 14." This originated as an after-dinner doggerel battle that lasted well into the night. The ballad concerns a ragged and hapless tramp printer who shows up at the newspaper office (apparently the actual office of the *Saint Joseph Gazette* where Field and Visscher worked).

> Why, sir, when there came in a wedding report,
> You ought to have seen that "lead-pounder" cavort!
> He got so confused, and so reckless beside,
> That for "kissing" he set "The groom pissed on the bride!"

In 1888 Vissch returned to the West Coast becoming editorial writer for the *Portland Oregonian,* then editor in chief of the Tacoma daily *Globe,* then the *Fairhaven Herald* in 1890.

A reviewer said of him, and his history of the Pony Express: "A terrible liar, a drunkard, a bad poet and a rascal, Visscher bore an amazing resemblance to comedian W. C. Fields." His close friend, Opie Read recalled an instance in a Chicago store when Visscher, concluding that some young women were giggling about his nose, rebuked them in this fashion: "I've owned better people than you are — owned them, sold them and spent the money for liquor, by God." *Vissch,* from which the following is extracted, was his first collection of sketches, published while he was editor of the *Saint Joseph Gazette.*

SMALL PICA.

A Printer's Story.

SOMEBODY HAS TOLD US THAT "the child is father to the man," & I am not going to dispute the orthodoxy of this back-action axiom, though I tremble at the responsibility which rests upon the godless children who begat this perverse generation.

APOLLYONIC.

It is not pertinent to my subject to inquire what other men may be. All the world knows that the printer, in the innocence of his youth, is nothing more nor less than a "devil;" and it is not unknown to many that the average adult product is a true chip of the old block — or, rather, the old chip amplified into a prodigious block.

LONG AGO.

In the modest virtue of my youth, when the evil days came not, I cherished, with other innocents, a decent respect for the art preservative, and deemed its votaries the autocrats of trades-men. I didn't realize, then, that the same power that lifts a mortal to the skies, might drag an angel down. In those hal-cyon days I knew a boy — I fear he was a devil — who wrought in a printing office. I didn't know exactly what his functions were, but remember that I always thought he brought away more ink on his face and hands than his employers could well afford to lose. This young typographical error, whose Chris-tian name was Jake, was quite an oracle among us, and often did he beguile us of our smiles as he recounted the marvel-ous sayings and doings of the printer-men, as we sat upon the slanting cellar-door of my father's mansion. It was rumored among us that Jake himself had been occasionally made the hero of their practical whims — once, in particular, when a jocund typo dispatched him to an office at the other end of the town for some italic commas; but he didn't tell us about this, and I didn't blame him for his animosity against the devil at the other office for letting that cat out of the bag.

JOHN SMITH.

At that early period of my history I shared, with all fools, both young and old, the desire to see my name in print, and Jake, with a benevolence which amounted to magnanimity in my eyes, volunteered to make me happy.

"Of course he could do it. What did I take him for? Would I have it set up in forty-line Pica Arabesque, or Double-Great Primer Ionic?"

Mystified at his erudition, I commended him to his own judgment in the matter; and that night the faithful demon produced from his trowsers pocket the talismanic type, organized and disciplined into the expression of "John Smith," all securely tied up with a string. The type appeared to me to be arranged in a semi-up-and-down fashion, but Jake said it would come out all right in print. He told me that the printers stood on their heads when they read the types, but I didn't believe that, even then.

Next day I went into the printing business on my own hook, and "John Smith" adorned innumerable books and articles of apparel belonging the Smith family, especially my shirt. It would have done the soul of Pochahontas good to have seen that shirt. The collar, the bosom, the back and the front, proclaimed my ownership, and I fear the tail came in for a share of the embellishment. I wouldn't print another edition of that shirt for a five-dollar bill. I couldn't afford to lose a shirt then any more than I can now, and I felt that no man, unless he was blind, could appropriate that shirt by mistake. My mother, however, frowned upon my enterprise, and pied my apparatus, thus knocking my earliest typographical venture in the head.

PI!

One fine morning in winter — or it may have been in summer — I was passing the office in which Jake was employed. It was early, and I peeped in. There was my friend wrestling manfully with a broom. He was alone and bade me enter, which I did, and immediatcly began making investigations. Type, presses, and all the mystic paraphernalia of the craft were duly inspected and handled without any startling accidents. On the stones were pages of all sizes and on all subjects. Jake told me some of them appertained to an algebra, then "in press," and volunteered to show me how the printers lifted them. He grappled a large page and handled it as easy as I would a brick, in fact a little too easily, as it turned out, for one of his dexterous movements resulted in an imminent deadly breach. I heard something drop, and the ghastly expression of Jake's countenance proclaimed the extent of the disaster. I recommended my unfortunate friend to run away, and go a-whaling, or enlist for a drummer in the army, and then I incontinently decamped. Not being of a romantic disposition, however, Jake remained and faced the melancholy music. His Saturday night's spending money was circumscribed in the immediate future, though whether his experiment with the algebra had anything to do with it or not I can only guess.

THE FATAL STEP.

Well, in the course of human events it becomes necessary for my parents, and sponsors in baptism, to place me in a position of usefulness, and Fate cast my lot among the types. I don't know why, but I suppose it was because I didn't know enough for anything else. Time went on as though nothing had happened, as it usually does; and after many kicks and cuffs, and curses, I became an adept in the manipulation of the leaden liars. I didn't sweep out any more nor run errands, and I revelled in my dignity. The boys used to yell "paste" at me as I went past them, for your untutored urchin always associates the noble art preservative with the book-binding interest, in his vulgar mind. But I had done the same thing in my innocent days, and though I fear I did not forgive them, I refrained from retaliation.

The printers in our office were of the staid and sober sort, who would never set a river on fire, and I don't believe they would have tried to put it out if some aspiring youth had fired it, and but for the occasional visit of a "thorough-bred" from the metropolis of the hemisphere I fear I should have been spoiled in the baking, and settled down into that vulgar, domestic, common-place nonentity, an honest man.

TRAMPS.

All the "tramps" in those days hailed from New York. I suppose they thought that was a recommendation. Our foreman was a queer old chap. He knew a great deal, but not half as much as he thought he did. He'd put a fellow at work on the worst manuscript he could find, and if he proved to be a "stoughton-bottle"* he was profanely recommended to agricultural pursuits. If, however, the visiting brother proved to be a skillful artisan he was petted and made much of until the morning after the first pay day, when we were apt to learn that the wayfarer had pursued his journey into the bowels of the land, or, more likely, a mournful message from the calaboose would repeat the oft-told tale.

---

* Stoughton-bottle = A dark green or black bottle formerly used for Dr Stoughton's bitters, shaped like a log cabin and used in the presidential campaign of 1840. The term from its association has come to imply a stupid person or a figurehead (*Cass City Chronicle*, September 8, 1939).

"THE THOROUGH-BRED."

"Yes distinctly I remember
It was in the bleak December"*

When a distinguished meteor flashed across our sky. This illustrious cosmopolitan came direct from the great city. Busy
tongues had sounded his praises in advance, and the evidences
of skill which he gave us did not belie his fame. He told me that
work was plenty in New York, that he had just resigned a "sit"
on the *Herald*. I wondered then why he left so nice a place, but
I could give a good guess now. His costume, too, troubled me.
He wore an overcoat which was not in the bloom of youth, to
be sure, but good enough for any one. Beneath it was a summer
vest, which had probably once been white. One boot — number 17 — adorned his right foot, while the left was encased in a
tattered slipper that would have raised bunions on the foot of
Cinderella. His tile was of the stove-pipe persuasion, but it was
plain that his head was not its original occupant, but a few cop-
ies of the *Journal* ingeniously sandwiched into the lining kept
it in its place. His eyes were bloodshot and his step unsteady,
but there was a devil-may-care tone of dignity in his style that
had magic in its impudence.

THE ELEPHANT.

I took a fancy to Tom from the start, and he returned my friendship. He did me the favor to borrow one of my shirts, and I
cordially recommended him to my aunt, who kept a boarding
house. Saturday night arrived as it always does, and I took him
out to see the town. We didn't get along as fast as I could have
wished; we had too many stoppages to make. The fact is my
friend Tom — as he told me at least — was anxious to know
where the best gin cocktails were compounded, with a view
to giving the fortunate establishment his permanent custom,

---

* Oft-parodied line from "The Raven" by Poe.

and if my money had have held out I think he would have been successful. We had a seven-by-nine theatre in our town, and I wanted to go there, but my metropolitan friend told me that my favorite actors were bloody sticks, and that I should go with him to the Bowery and see Kirby when I came to New York, and so we went and took another gin cocktail. I didn't hanker after this last imbibation, but I wouldn't for the world expose my weakness to my illustrious friend.

The following hours of that eventful night are a little chaotic in my memory now. I only remember being jostled and towsled in the very giddy mazes of a wicked dance; that sailors of every nation, and wantons of every hue, surrounded me; that they all seemed to me to be frightfully drunk; my cosmopolitan companion kicked up a muss in which I was speedily engulfed; that a robust female assaulted me with a vigor and pertinacity worthy a better cause; that in my forced departure from that haunt of vice, I received a parting salute from a toe, that was neither light nor fantastic, which boosted me into the arms of a friendly watchman, who, out of respect for my relatives and the promise of a subsidy, guided me to the paternal doorstep.

AFTER THE BATTLE.

The gin-cocktails had done their legitimate work, and I was as sober as an owl that had never been boiled. Stealthily I stole to my once virtuous chamber, and with trembling hand ignited a lucifer and caused the light to shine. My too faithful mirror revealed to my clouded vision a sight which horrified me. I thought of the fellow who went down from Jerusalem to Jericho and fell among thieves, and wondered if he looked as bad as I did. I doubt it to this day.

I didn't go to Sunday School next day, but the doctor came and put me together. He had accouched me and was used to me. He told my mother I had been drinking, though I don't think the dear soul believed it. I was thankful that my jaw was broken, as under the circumstances I couldn't be reasonably expected to give my version of the story.

I had plenty of time and food for reflection. My estimate of "thoroughbreds" was considerably reduced by this little episode. I was not quite sure, but seemed to have a dim remembrance of seeing my esteemed friend hurry into the street at the commencement of the engagement, and I wondered why he did it. Perhaps he was afraid of seriously injuring some of the jolly tars, and suppressed his anger on philanthropic grounds, but why he didn't take me with him was not quite so clear. Perhaps that was the way they did it in New York.

INGRATITUDE.

Youth and strong poultices pulled me through, and with a guilty conscience and a sheepish gait, I reported for duty one fine morning. The unfeeling brutes had no compassion upon my misery. The very "devil" poked his incipient jokes at me. On inquiry I learned that my festive friend from the city had "jumped the town" soon after my misfortune. The day he left he borrowed ten dollars from the foreman to send to his wife who was sick. This he learned from a telegraphic dispatch which he displayed with tears in his eyes. I have the best of reasons for believing that the whole thing was a ruse. My aunt, who kept the boarding-house, called on me at the office and gave me a withering lecture before the whole crowd. She informed me that she would call again and that I should pay her to the uttermost farthing, and she meant it. But I didn't.

I KICK.

It was getting warm for me at home, and I took a desperate resolution. I kept my own counsel, gathered together a few dollars, packed my "kista,"* and quietly stole away. Proudly, but not

---

* kista = chest; Swedish word for coffin

without anxiety, I landed at Peekslip, and immediately made my way to the favorite haunts of the jovial typographers. I was a trifle flush, and immediately became a favorite with the "second board" (a numerous class of needy, lazy and vicious typos who never work, but lay for such gudgeons as I was). They all gave me encouragement, though none of them seemed to have anything to do themselves. The skies looked so bright that I didn't consider it necessary to go to work right away, and so, after paying a week's board to a Dutchman in William street, I rolled around with the boys.

"CARRYING THE BANNER."

You may not believe it, but those fellows stuck to me till my pockets were empty, and my silver watch, Sunday clothes, and all the collateral I possessed had "gone where the woodbine twineth." The Dutchman booted me out as soon as my week was up, and for the first time in my life I found myself in a hostile emporium "carrying the banner."

About that time my old friend Tom dropped into town. He was in a hilarious mood when I saw him. He appeared to enjoy my misfortunes; asked me how all the fools in my town were getting along; requested me to send his love to my aunt, and "shook" me without asking me to take even a gin cocktail. But I had my revenge on him in later years. I met him one day in a state of extreme dilapidation and misery, and gave him the price of four drinks at Schnaederbeck's — one shilling. Thus did I heap coals of fire upon his head.

ROUNDERS.

I hustled around and found a companion in misery. We swore fidelity to each other, and each went his way to look for work. Fortune favored me, and that night I had a home and a job. If I forgot to share my good luck with my miserable friend, I had no doubt he would have done the same by me, and so my conscience was eased. Things went on swimmingly for a while. I got acquainted with numerous "rounders," the narrative of whose haps and mishaps would fill the British museum. I fear a recital of their exploits would not be wholesome reading for the rising generation, unless one could contrive to graft a dismal moral upon the tail end.

I FLY BY NIGHT.

I suppose that every one knows that a cosmopolitan printer, when in his normal condition, is dead broke. Creditors are always hard-hearted. Why, I've had a fellow to stand and talk to me for half an hour about a matter of ten dollars or so that I owed him. This is not pleasant to the victim, and when a chap has to go half a mile out of his way to get his dinner, in order to escape the importunities of these scoundrels, any reasonable man will consider him justifiable in absquatulating. So, one morning I woke up in the Quaker City perfectly solvent. I didn't owe a cent there, and I had no hard feelings against my creditors in New York. I forgave them from the bottom of my heart.

The printer's boulevard, then known as the Barbary Coast, presented the usual attractions. The war was going on at that time, and before long Uncle Sam did me the honor to draft me into his service. I didn't owe allegiance to the State of Pennsylvania, whatever I might owe to its citizens, and, so having no stomach for the fight, and no means to emigrate with, I wrote myself a "pass" to Washington. It worked.

ROUGH ON SMITH.

In the Federal city I came across an old acquaintance whom I shall call Dick. I more than suspected that Dick had defrauded the nation of his martial services — that he had "jumped the bounty" on divers occasions, though I don't think the military arm of the service lost much by it. Dick played a little trick on me thus wise: We were both working one day on the *Chronicle*, when a disguised minion of the army put in an appearance. Dick stood nearest the door, and the disguised minion approached him with:

"Is Dick working here?"

"Yes, that's him," said Dick, pointing to me. Whereupon the *gen d'arme* stepped up to your humble servant and said, "old man, you are wanted at the guard house!"

Have you any idea of how it feels to be struck by lightning? I had then. I hadn't heard his conversation with Dick. I thought of the Philadelphia draft, and visions of a thousand Bull Runs whirled through my brain. But my captor was in a hurry, and at the door I was surrounded by a squad of heroes whose sanguinary bayonets gleamed in the sunlight. Sadly and sorrowfully I obeyed the corporal's order to "fall in," and handcuffed to a bushwhacker, who had the bulk of a mastodon and the countenance of a polar bear, I filed down Pennsylvania avenue and Seventh street, and took boat for Alexandria, where we were debouched into a pen that would have shamed the Andersonville stockade, and left to chew the cud of very bitter fancy. Morning came and we were mustered into line and told to answer to our names. My heart was in my throat during that fearful ordeal. I couldn't have answered if my name had been called; but, strange as it may seem, the name of John Smith didn't appear upon that roll of infamy. I noticed that the name of my friend Dick was called to which no one answered, and thought I saw the point. The sergeant came round and insisted that I was Dick, but I wouldn't stand that. I told him that I was anxious to serve my country but was not willing that my glory should go to the credit of another. In the course of a week or so I proved my identity, when after marching me down a dozen regimental lines and finding that none of them would claim me as a deserter, they kindly permitted me to walk back through the mud to Washington.

As I had surmised, so soon as Dick saw my inglorious exit by the front door, he lost no time in getting to the Baltimore depot by way of the rear. I met him afterward in Cincinnati. He was too flush for a respectable printer, but he "whacked up" and I forgave him. He even had the impudence to make this odious proposition to me: He would go and join a New Jersey regiment into which the science of reading and writing had not penetrated. He would become principal letter-writer and scribe. When the paymaster came around he would write their letters home enclosing the greenbacks. These he would direct to me at Cincinnati and the "Spaniards" would never know the difference until he had found means to take "French leave" and join me. I admired the rascal's implicit confidence in my honesty, but indignantly spurned the idea of defrauding my valiant countrymen. I suppose I ought to have shot him on the spot. But I didn't. I let him go.

I met an old "pard" in the Queen City. He had been the rounds, and I tackled him for a narrative of his adventures. I "throwed a bowl or two into him," and he revealed himself as follows:

THE TALE OF MY BEARDED PARD.

The straits to which the itinerant, or wild goose portion of the "art preservative," who fly South in winter, and East, North and West in summer, may be illustrated by the following boarding-house experience: The trouble is as apt to stare an honest, though trunkless, typo in the face, as an adept board-jumper. Arriving from Nashville in the fall of 18—, at Louisville, I found work very scarce, and having no Saratoga, I received so many rebuffs from victimized landladies that I had "carried the banner" for several days. At last I became desperate, as also a partner chip I had picked up, and we agreed to start out in search of a boarding house, promising each other if either was successful to bring the other a "lunch," telling the landlady that we were to work that night. I took a street I had not been on before, and went a great distance; I espied a boarding house, which, by its modest appearance and suburban location, I hoped had not received patronage from any printer. Vain hope! I was ushered into a sitting room by the landlord; for this I felt relieved, as, in my hungry condition I did not want to look at a woman, much less, speak to one. I told the man I wanted to engage board. All right, he said; what business did I follow; was I a stranger in the city, etc. I told him I was a stranger, and that I was a printer. At the mention of the word printer he seemed to swell to the proportions of a giant, his face became fiery, and he simply looked hideous.

"Printer! Well, by G—d!" he said. "I've boarded a good many of your calling, and, d—n me, if I ever saw an honest one yet!" He then commenced ransacking his side-pocket, and presently pulled out a note, written in pencil, at the sight of which I was much relieved, as visions of pistols for one flashed through my brain.

"There," said he, "read that!" I did as requested. The note ran:

"Mr. ———: I will surely pay you the $25 I owe you to-morrow.

"(Signed)   J. B."

The writer of this note was my partner, who had started out when I did to find a house.

The landlord said, "That's a printer! Do you know him?" I told him no. He continued: "That fellow made $35 last week and never gave me a cent!" I told him I had just arrived from Nashville, and that I did not know him, and if that was the kind of person he was, I should take care not to get acquainted with him. At the mention of Nashville, his tone changed, and he melted, as all Tennesseeans do, at the name of their birthplace; he said he was born in Nashville, but left 30 years before. Here was my last hope; I told him I was also born in Nashville about the time he left; I named the street I was brought to light on, which he remembered well; I descanted on the sin of abolition, and the virtues of Robinson County white whisky, etc., until I won him. I took the lunch to my pard, and sat up until one o'clock at night, and then went to my lodgings. It was necessary to sit up late to lead the people at the house to think I was at work. It is needless to say that my partner did not fare as well as I did, as he was well known in the city, and had "lifted" all the available boarding houses. I succeeded in getting a few days' work, and paid my bill, for which I received the heartfelt thanks of the landlord, who frankly told me that he thought I would "beat" him; but he said he had never turned a Tennesseean from his door, and never would.

While meandering through the interior of Missouri, I became "stuck" in a small town where there were two little weeklies. I went to one of the offices and asked for work, I wished to work enough to reach St. Louis by rail. They had no work. Now, all city printers have a holy horror of pulling a hand-press — no matter how much they may have done it in their younger days. The proprietor of this office told me that the "jour" at the other office was sick, and it was publication day, and if I would go over there the proprietor would in all probability, employ me to work off the paper, which, otherwise, he would have to do himself. I told him I couldn't stand it. He then said if I could convince the other editor that I could not work the press, he might let me set some type for the next paper; and with the characteristic love of one country editor for his nearest brother of the scissors and quill, he helped me to "put up a job" on him. We procured a piece of beefsteak and saturated a rag with blood, and tied up my left hand — taking care to adjust a "stick" into it, so that I could set type, but could not work press, I called on the rival editor. Yes, he wanted a man right away to work off the edition — the safety of the country depended upon the appearance of which — I essayed to work the press. At the first turn of the wheel I gave an unearthly screech. I then explained to him that I had fallen from the cars and cut my hand exactly where the pressure of the handle came. I regretted this

very much, as I was in need of money to reach St. Louis — the
haven for the present — where every tramp has a "sure thing"
on getting work. He took the bait, and I went to piling up Long
Primer for the next week's crusher. The affair pleased the first
editor so well that he added to my exchequer to the amount
of $2, the only money, as he declared, he had taken in for six
weeks.

REFLECTIONS.

And here let me speak a kind word for the pioneer country
editor of the west. Usually he is a printer with a family; he is
a city bred printer, and leaves the city reluctantly simply because he cannot support his family in the manner he thinks he
should. He leaves the city reluctantly with his treasures, well
knowing he is to bury himself for a term of years. If, by delving,
hard work and hard living, and poor pay, he at last emerges
from the chrysalis of a murky printing office and becomes a
full blown legislator and law maker of his adopted State — as
frequently occurs — do not, gentle reader, imagine that his has
been a smooth and tranquil road to preferment. Far from it!
He has worked for all he has gained. Having made this stride
in advancement, he becomes a useful citizen, beloved by all
who know him, and an oracle — to a greater or less degree —
in the immediate neighborhood of his home. Very often, too,
this useful member of frontier life is not a printer, but a smart,
go-ahead half-paid city reporter, generally urged to "go west,"
by the same domestic pride. All honor to the western country
editor!

SHOULD AULD ACQUAINTANCE BE FORGOT.

The beer in Cincinnati is above reproach, but the Dutch don't
give it away. Things had been rather mixed and I was in a
strange country, laboring under a pressure of pecuniary li-
abilities. Starvation stared me unblushingly in the face, and

the chilly blasts of approaching Winter sported roughly with my nankeen habiliments. I couldn't go South without a musket, and I never could learn the manual of arms. Despairingly I stalked into a popular beer saloon one afternoon in October, to rest myself and read the papers.

I had scarcely entered the door when a stentorian voice yelled out, "Hello! Joe, by jingo! I've been looking for you all day," and a jovial looking country gentleman seized me by both hands. "Joe, it's good for the eyes to see you; come, take a drink," continued he. I was about to undeceive my cordial friend when the last sentence struck upon my ear. I couldn't do it then, without injustice to myself; so I cheerfully drank bumpers to his health. He asked me when I left home. I told him I hadn't been at home for some time, which seemed to satisfy him. He kindly inquired about Eli and the girls. I informed him that they were well so far as I knew, and we quaffed a bowl to their health. I dreaded any more catechising, and was about to plead a special engagement and tear myself away, when he launched out "I got a letter from Sally a spell ago; here it is, read it."

Conscious of my villainy I took the letter and read it. The superscription was John W. B. ——, Richmond, Indiana. It was dated from Lancaster, Pennsylvania, a town in which I had stopped. I had found out my friend's name, and the place of my residence, when at home, and I felt satisfied that if we didn't meet any more of our old acquaintances, that I could manage John, at least until he got sober. I inquired about Richmond and talked affectionately of Lancaster. John invited me to his hotel to supper and I couldn't refuse such an esteemed friend. After supper we went to the theatre. Between the acts of course we went across the street to see a man. I didn't like to see John spending all the money, and I told him so. It really hurt my feelings. I had left my pocketbook at home, and John kindly relieved me of my embarrassment by the loan of a ten dollar note. The old boy was getting a little too noisy for the theatre by this time and I coaxed him to go home, which he did, and I hied me to the Indianapolis depot without delay. I respect that gentleman to this day, and no one shall say aught against him in my presence.

POOR JAKE.

Indianapolis is a very good town to go to, and an excellent town to come from. In this town, for the first time since boyhood, I met my old friend Jake. I regret to say that Jake looked care-worn and really he was so starved and emaciated that his clothes didn't fit him, though I don't think they were ever made for him. His head was as big as ever. I am not sure but that he was suffering from the "swell-head." The deep blue shading around his left eye he told me came from a fall, but the boys in town said that the fall was a subsequent affair, and that Jake landed on his back. Notwithstanding his misfortunes I embraced him and that night I went to bed jolly. The next morning I remonstrated with Jake upon his dissipation and riotous living. He acknowledged the corn, though I believe he alluded sarcastically to one of our old Sunday School lessons about a beam in somebody's eye. Nevertheless we took an "eye-opener," swore off and went to work. We stuck to our resolution faithfully until Saturday when Jake complained of the stomach-ache. I feared it was caused by the greenbacks in his pocket, but I absolved him from his oath for this once, and recommended blackberry brandy. He didn't like to drink alone, so to make the thing fair and square, I joined him.

Monday's sun rose upon a cloudless sky. I awoke from a troubled slumber, and felt in my pockets. Just as I expected; Jake in the calaboose and nothing in the treasury. To cap the climax we had forgotten to go to work Sunday night, and our nails were driven in at the office. I got a reporter to get Jake out of the "boose," and after holding a solemn council of deliberation, we decided to take the turnpike for Lafayette.

ON THE PRAIRIE.

Never shall I forget that dismal march. Night found us on the road and no town in sight. The roosters crowed, the geese cackled, and yelping curs followed us from farm house to farm house. Jake was in favor of putting up for the night in a friendly hay-stack. He was used to it and didn't seem to mind it, but visions of vigilance committees, horse-thieves, long ropes and short shrifts had bothered me, and we pushed on to Jimtown. It was not late, and we knocked at the door of an humble mansion. Three men, four women, and about sixteen children answered our knock, accompanied by the inevitable yellow dog.

THE POWER OF ELOQUENCE.

It had been arranged that Jake should do the talking, but his heart failed him, and I came to his relief. I told them that we were rebel prisoners who had taken the amnesty oath and been released from Rock Island, and that we had been forced into the army, much against our will; that we expected to find friends in Cincinnati. I hope I shall be forgiven for it, but I actually told them that I had been conscripted from a Southern college when I was studying for the ministry. I struck it that time. They asked me the denomination of my creed. I wickedly replied: "Methodist." I struck it again. I discovered that they were of that persuasion, and as I had attended several camp-meetings, I hoped to pass a theological muster. We were invited in. As the light fell upon Jacob's left eye I shuddered. The black was nearly gone, but that indescribable blending of colors which always accompanies the convalesence of a bunged eye remained. It was anything but a Methodist eye. My genius came again to the rescue. I told them that for the expression of Union sentiments, we had been cruelly beaten by our comrades, and called on Jake's eye as a witness. They gave us food to eat, and when we had done I examined their phrenological developments, and told them fearful stories of our campaigns, which I had read in the newspapers. I obtained agricultural employment for Jacob, and received a pressing invitation to stay over Sunday and preach for them. That night we slept in a comfortable bed, and after breakfast in the morning, I went out to see the town. I signalled Jake from the field, and that night we walked into Lafayette.

I WANT TO GO TO CHICAGO.

Here I "shook" Jake. His propensity for a country life didn't suit me. There was nothing that he could find to do, but I left him sitting in a printing office, and meandered down to the junction. I had fixed my gaze on Chicago. A train came along. I couldn't resist the temptation, so jumped into the front car, and eagerly set about concocting a yarn for the conductor. He came at last.

"Ticket, Sir."

I arose and commenced my story. I think he saw the gist, for he said: "Where do you want to go to?"

"I want to go to Chicago, sir, but I have been robbed of all my money —"

"Get off at the next station," and he passed on. We flew along to the next station, and I got off. It was a dreary place, and just as the train was moving off I got on again, and resumed my former seat. It was a long time before the captain came around again, but he came at last, and gazed at me with astonishment.

"I thought I told you to get off at the first station."

"Yes sir," I replied, in my most innocent manner. "I did get off there, but the man in the office told me that was not Chicago. I thought you had made a mistake, and so I got on again."

The people in my vicinity smiled, and the conductor looked nonplussed. He passed on, to get a club I supposed, to assassinate me with, but he didn't come back, and I rode on to Chicago. I should be sorry to read in the papers of a rail-road accident in which that worthy official had passed in his checks.

A NOBLE SOLDIER.

Chicago is a noble city. It reminds one of New York. Something is always liable to turn up in Chicago. I was sitting in a barber's chair in that city, one day; an American citizen of African descent was lazily scratching my head. I was thinking of home. People sometimes will think of home you know. In the other chair reclined an officer of our then veteran army. He signalled a supernumerary octoroon, and told him to go into the saloon next door and bring him some whisky. I'm sure he said whisky, and I looked around at the familiar word, and the warrior, who was slightly fuddled, invited me to join him. Not wishing to offend him, I accepted his invitation. This little courtesy brought on a conversation, and we took a walk together. I am not sure but that we took something else. I told him I was from New York, and wouldn't be sorry if I was back again. "Come with me," said my martial friend, "I'm going to take a lot of prisoners on to-morrow, and I can lump you in amongst them, just as well as not." I gazed upon him with admiration. I said to him, "Colonel" — I think he was a second lieutenant — "Colonel, are you liable to change your mind?" He laughed at my suspicion; said an American soldier's word was as good as his bond, and the landlord filled the flowing bowl. We made a night of it, and ere the next day's sun had reached its meridian I was ostensibly a political prisoner, bound for Fort Lafayette.

THE BROAD GAUGE.

It is pleasant to ride on a broad-gauge road. The Erie is one of them. The passengers on that road are all Christians. My unfortunate position as a prisoner, my blighted youth and gushing innocence excited the warmest sympathy. One benevolent gentleman — may he live long and prosper — promised to see Mr. Lincoln in my behalf, for which I tendered him my most grateful and even tearful thanks. An amiable female of ancient mien, endeavored to cheer me; she gave me a quarter-section of ginger-bread, and two Abolition tracts from her reticule. She asked me if my friends were wealthy, I told her they were stripped of all. She thought money would be of no use to me in my confinement. I thought differently. She wore several valuable rings on her fingers, and I ventured to ask her for a souvenir — something which should ever remind me of her angelic charity. The sympathetic creature endowed me with a lock of her venerable hair. I could have got ten dollars on the ring at Simpson's; he wouldn't give a cent for the hair, but I took it with profuse acknowledgements, and threw it out of the window the first opportunity I could obtain to do so, unobserved.

AN ACCIDENTAL ESCAPE.

Reaching Port Jervis I jumped out to invest my last dime. I patronized a gentleman of German extraction, his hostelrie being the first that met my view. I had scarcely grasped the demijohn when the lubberly Teuton remarked:

"You bedder hurry up; you gid laift."

I sprang to the door. The treacherous train was gliding gracefully along the broad-gauge, about a quarter of a mile away.

"Get left! you son of a bologna sausage! I am left."

I've been at Grand Junction, Mississippi, all night. I've resided at Napoleon, Arkansas, and tasted the pleasures of social life, at Julesburg, on wheels, but Port Jervis floored me. I told the station master that I was a political prisoner, sentenced to be hung; that the circumstances of the case required that I should be executed in New York; that it was his duty as a truly loyal man, to give me a ticket to go on the next train. He derisively told me to go to a place which I won't name, but which is said to be excessively warm all the year round, and I censured him for his profanity, whereupon he pointed to the door and lifted his dexter hoof, clad in a number nine cowhide boot. As a hint always was as good as a kick to me, if not better, I departed without further hesitation.

I went over and toasted my shins by the Dutchman's fire, and interviewed him with regard to dinner, exposed my impecuniosity and tried to work upon his sympathies. He pointed to a pile of wood in front of the door, and in heathenish pantomime insinuated that I should earn my bread by the sweat of my brow. Shades of the Know-Nothings are we to stand this? I gave him a look of scornful pity, and went back to the depot. I boarded the next train and took the front seat in the front car. The conductor starts at the back end. He came and I told him the political prisoner story. He asked me if I took him for a fool. I didn't dare to tell him the truth, but endeavored by a soft answer to turn away his wrath. He threw me off at Patterson. I took the cattle train for Communipaw, and once more looked upon the spires of Trinity and St. Paul's.

Now I have entirely reformed. I have settled with all my creditors including my aunt, who kept the boarding-house, and would not, under any circumstances, have placed these memoirs in the hands of the rising generation, except as a terrible illustration of the effects of learning the black art of printing.

J. J. McDaid: What's In A Name?

A Rose by Any Other Name
Would Smell as Sweet.

AMONG THE COUNTLESS TYPOGRAPHICAL TOURISTS whose names adorn the payrolls of every prominent Journal from the Penobscot to the Colorado there are many whose legal cognomens are unknown even to their most intimate friends.

About ten years ago R. H. Watts and Sam Alley were practicing pedestrianism along the dreary confines of the Mojave desert. The professional tour through the land of the Montezuma had been unsuccessful, and their wardrobe had been sadly depleted by the ravages of time and the persistency of the frontier landlords. By one of those fortuitous streaks that appear providential, on nearing The Needles they discovered a pair of discarded pantaloons. These necessary articles had seen brighter days, but their condition, though unsuited to ostentatious display — that is, they would not harmonize with a dress-suit — were much superior to those possessed by Mr. Watts. He therefore determined to profit by fortune's favors, and accordingly donned the garment. On arriving at The Needles Watts was greeted with amazement by the denizens of that tropic burg, who vociferously cried, "Tom! Tom!" Alley determined to investigate the cause of this apparently inexplicable familiarity. To his infinite surprise he discovered, painted on the leg of Watts' dudish trousers in large old gold letters, the name "Tom." On reaching Los Angeles Alley related the incident, and R. H. Watts has since been "Tom." Watts will give the reader fuller details.

John R. Lamson, at one time Treasurer of this Union, President of Washoe and Eureka (Nev.) Unions, and now of Washington, D. C., where he has just finished a term as First Vice-President of Columbia Union, is known as "Spotted Tail." "Spot" was a noted raconteur, and many a pleasant evening was spent by the boys in listening to his superb drawing of the long-bow. During one of his entertaining moods he related a perilous adventure in the Gunnison country, which resulted in his capture by the Indians. He eventually secured his release by instructing the redoubtable *sachem* "Spotted Tail" in the mysteries of "Kema" (Indian poker). This incident, which was received with incredulous glances by the boys, was the origin of "Spot's" title. A German who kept a store on one of the prominent corners in a town in which Lamson was working some years after entered the office one evening and asked the first man he met for Mr. Lamson. He was informed that no such man worked there. The Teuton was not satisfied, as he had been informed to the contrary. To satisfy him, the compositor named the men in the office, and when he came to Lamson he called him "Mr. Spot." The merchant departed, not knowing that "Spot" and Lamson were the same.

Charlie Latimer, who is known to every printer on the Coast, and whose eventful career as actor, composer, preacher and tramp is also well known, fell heir, at the hands of Henry Duffy, to the title of "Soap." In his career as theatrical manager, etc., he always carried a bar of soap. He said it was his wardrobe when he was a tramp printer, and he would continue to wear it. And so he does. To this day he is known as "Soap" Latimer. While paying one of his customary trips to the Comstock, Latimer became acquainted with the typographical wag of that section, who presented him with an acrostic emblematic of his various callings, which ran something like this:

> L is for lend me a quarter, you know;
> A is for acting wherever I go;
> T is for trust me for a week's board;

I is for industry which I have not adored;
M is for meals, denoted the "square";
E is for eating when I get there;
R is for rustling, both early and late —
— the whole is for Latimer, the only, the Great.

George W. Hoffman, who came to this Coast from Michigan fourteen years ago, brought with him an exact imitation of the calliope. Place Hoffman in a room unseen, and let him start in, and the listener could imagine himself floating down the Mississippi to the entrancing strains of the never-to-be-forgotten calliope. For this he is to-day called "Toots." One day in Virginia, Nevada, "Toots" was unfortunate enough to witness "a man prepared for breakfast."

When the case came up he was a witness, and, as his name was about the middle of the list, he threw himself lazily into a chair, and, placing his hands before his eyes, began to dream. Retrospectively his mind wandered back to boyhood's sunny days. The scenes of early youth passed in panoramic view before him, and once again he roamed his native heath, careless and free. The stentorian tones of the Clerk, as he syllabled the name of G. W. Hoffman, elicited no response from "Toots." He occasionally glanced up to note the more than ordinary commotion, then sank back in blissful reverie. The Clerk called again. The Judge, noting Hoffman looking up unheedingly to the call, assessed him $25 for contempt. But "Toots" still failed to respond. The Clerk became exasperated at Hoffman's apparent ignoring of the summons, and remarked, "What's the matter? Don't you know you are being called?" "Really," said Hoffman, "was he calling me? I had actually forgotten my own name." The Judge, discovering the absence of intent, remitted the fine.

Max Rothschild, General Superintendent of the *Daily Report,* some three years ago, upon learning that the Jersey Lily was about to build a house of ancient architecture at the Mission, went her one better by erecting on the highest point on Bernal Heights a palatial mansion. In his eagerness to outdo the Lily he overreached himself, as it soon became manifest that to live with any safety in his costly structure it was necessary to brace it with ropes, and it now presents the appearance of a circus tent. Some of Rothschild's most intimate friends among the compositors of this city assert that when he arrives at the bottom of the mountain where he dwells he takes a balloon, and when he wants to descend he brings into requisition the modern parachute. But what has this to do with our story? Simply this: When the printers of the *Report*, who average 1,700 an hour, notwithstanding the noise which would make a foundry ashamed of itself that floats through the building, heard of Max's eccentric move, they unanimously decided to christen him "Baron," and if he were called anything else today he would feel insulted.

Wells Drury, who now pushes a Faber for the *Examiner*, and Jim Townsend and Olander E. Jones, owners of papers in different parts of Nevada, had their soubriquets when they graced the typographical ranks. Drury was known as "Little Bennie," Townsend as "Truthful James," which title he earned by his unwavering veracity, Jones was known as "Dan" a name he acquired while traveling with a circus as clown.

W. D. Perry of the *Alta* received his suggestive pseudonym of "Beg-off-Billie" from a propensity to get tired and "Corp" Saunders of the same paper earned his military title for active services in the Amador War.

Pete Meyers, though hardly 29 years of age, has been known for years by the strange name of "Old Pete."

McDaid, an Hibernian, was Secretary of the San Francisco Typographical Union, No. 21. On September 24, 1899 he was admitted to the Union Printers' Home in Colorado Springs, suffering from Phthisis. He was 38.

A TYPOGRAPHICAL TOURIST answering to the somewhat elaborate cognomen of "Michael Bejasus," struck this burg last Saturday on his way north. At Chouteau he was "horsed" out of the Pullman (unvarnished) with little ceremony and his pockets searched by the conductor and brakey. The indignity and not the loss was complained of.

✳✳✳

— HEARD FROM AGAIN: "Oscar Leonard put in an appearance, Sunday night, after a sojourn of about a year in Arkansas. If Peter B. Lee is really dead, it leaves Oscar the patriarch of Western typographical tourists. One thing that may be said in favor of Oscar is, that he does not often try to beat a railroad out of a ride. He is a good walker; and while he is too honest to make a practice of stealing rides, he regards it as a waste of money to pay fare." —Troy *Chief.*

— COPY WAS OUT. The devil picked up a paper and said. "Here's something about a woman — must I cut it out?" "No," thundered the editor, "the first disturbance ever created in the world was occasioned by the devil fooling about a woman."

✳✳✳

TYPOGRAPHICAL TOURISTS are said to be conspicuously numerous in Chippewa Falls. The Workman thinks a car full of them must have been let loose in that vicinity.

A Morning Caller.

"I WAS A GOOD BIT DRUNK when I struck town last Saturday," observed Reddy, the Typographical Tourist, as he drifted in the other day to shake hands with his old pal, the Judge, "and I loitered down to the depot just as the train happened to come in. I am so used to riding trains that I just kind of naturally swung up on to the top of a car, thinking to myself that Frank Finch would be expecting me at the Chautauqua about this time anyway. And so I composed myself to sleep, thinking to wake up in a little while in Ottawa. And the next thing I knew I was in Chanute, which I had only left two hours before. It is playing little jokes like that on myself that keeps me young. A man that travels a good deal in the way I do has queer experiences. For example I was dropping down between a couple of cars one night when the train stopped, when by bad luck my foot struck a lady's head instead of the platform rail. I had on a pair of wrong font shoes you know and of course they smashed the lady's hat instanter, and she let out a yell that you would have thought a pack of Comanche Indians were after her. I left in a great hurry, for if the people had caught me they would have murdered me.

"But talking about those wrong font shoes, that was all owing to the hard heart of a jailer over here in Missouri. It drives me to drink to go into Missouri, and this time I must have been more than usual loud and boisterous for they locked me up. And the next morning they told me I must go before the judge to answer for high crimes and misdemeanors.

"I looked at myself and while I am not overmuch finicky myself, yet I know what is due to authority, and so I said to myself,

'Reddy,' says I, 'You are in no shape, to go before the court in such clothes as these. It would be a disgrace to the profession.' And so I took them off and found some papers and a match and burned them. Well not having my trunks with me, of course, and not being exactly cut out for a bloomin' Venus, and being due in court at nine o'clock, why the jailer didn't see his way clear to carry out the instructions without providing me with a new suit, which he did all right until he came to the shoes and then he took it out on me by giving me these wrong-fonts, as you can see for yourself." And he held out for inspection two feet that were covered with very much mismated shoes.

"There are three classes of papers I won't work for," he resumed, "religious papers, temperance papers and Pop. papers. They are all on the bum. What I like is a man like Yoe, down at Independence. Soon as he sees you come into the shop, turns to his table and writes you out an order. — And he doesn't say 'Give this tramp a meal.' He says 'Please entertain this gentleman!' Make the hotel man think you *are* a gentleman! Yes sir, fools him! I'm not a tramp. I work when I have to, and I travel because I like to. I haven't got any folks. Nobody's calling me but the birds. Where do you think I slept last night? Out there under one of those trees. Slept like a child till seven o'clock this morning. And I didn't wake up in any dingy, stuffy room either. Woke up in God's temple, walls wider and pearlier than any palace, ceiling higher than any cathedral dome, birds singing sweeter than any choir, trees and the grass a prettier picture than Rafael ever painted. People that live in houses don't know what they miss. * * *

"Make it a quarter this time? Thanks. *Adios, hombre.*"

And he went away.

Reddy's Revenge.

THE SCENE WAS A SMALL Missouri town on the Mississippi river, a trifle more than one hundred miles north of St. Louis; the time — well, not twenty years ago. I was just out of my teens, and had a tolerable knowledge of the printing business. It was presidential year, and a heated campaign was on. I was publishing a six column folio morning paper set in long primer. The use of material and press I rented from one of the two weeklies of the town. *The Star* (I withhold the true name) was issued as a morning sheet because I was able to procure the St. Louis evening paper by express between 11 and 12 o'clock p.m. on the day of their publication, and by a judicious use of the shears gave our little public late telegraph news several hours in advance of the arrival of the next morning's city papers. This was my first — and last(?) — faking. Service by wire was out of the question.

I was proprietor, editor, reportorial staff and general hustler of *The Star*. The "force" consisted of three young men, one of whom performed the duties of foreman and make-up, and an apprentice. We knew nothing of unionism, and if a "chapel meeting" had been mentioned we would have started a hymn or taken up a collection.

One September afternoon, as I was preparing to go forth in the capacity of reporter, the foreman poked his head into the room which country editors delight to call the *sanctum,* & said:

"Tom just sent down word that he's got a chill and can't work tonight. I don't see how we'll fill her up unless you set considerable type yourself."

"Don't believe I can do much, Abe," I replied. "I've got to attend the Grassy Creek meeting, and can't get back before 10 o'clock. Do the best you can, and we'll fill up with ads. from the weekly."

I went to the meeting, which was a big blowout for *The Star*'s candidates. When it was over I drove to town as fast as a due regard for life and limb would permit. It lacked just ten minutes of 10 as I rushed into the office, exclaiming:

"Abe, you and Hank work away on that local news, and I'll set the meeting from my notes" — not an unusual proceeding with me in those days.

I threw off my coat and turned to the corner of the room in which the weekly frames stood, where I expected to find a pair of full cases. I was astounded, to state it mildly, at what I saw. Perched upon the only decent stool the office afforded, with my sweetbriar pipe in his mouth, was a stranger. He was distributing long primer at a high rate of speed.

I can close my eyes and see him now. He was the first of his kind I ever saw, and he impressed me so that I shall never forget him. He was nearly six feet in height as I learned when he got off the stool, with round shoulders; age, somewhere between thirty and fifty. His hair, which hadn't associated with a pair of shears for at least six months, was of that shade which the boys always spoke of as red, and his face was nearly covered with a shaggy beard and mustache of the same hue.

On one foot was a boot, on the other a shoe, both badly down at the heel and as rusty as a barndoor hinge. His trousers, which were inartistically fringed at the bottom, were held up by one "gallus" made of bed ticking. Waistcoat he had none. His coat, which hung at the end of the frame, was a double breasted frock that had once five or six years before I saw it been a handsome garment, but it had changed with years. How it did shine! On one side there was an entire absence of buttons. On the other side were two, one cloth covered and one of black horn, nearly as large as a silver dollar. I discovered later that when he wanted to button this wonderful coat and "brace up," as he called it, he used two little hickory skewers as substitutes for the absent buttons.

As I completed my survey of this queer looking individual he tossed the last letter in his hand into the cap G box, turned on the stool, puffed a cloud of "Missouri lugs" smoke half across the room, and said in a great primer voice:

"Hullo, boss! You've been slid tonight, and I'm on extras. I ain't much on good looks; I'm a little off my feet just now; but I can stand type on end faster'n a foundry can cast it, and I haven't seen a proof since I got out o' my time. Want to see my card?"

I didn't know just what reply to make to this odd speech, but after hesitating a moment I said "Yes."

He reached for that wonderful double breasted frock, and diving down into the skirt pocket drew forth what had once been a piece of white bristol board, about the size of an ordinary business card. Though it had held its own on size and was still bristol, it looked as if it had received an impression from a heavily inked tint block representing a North river fog. Minus the tint here is the card:

> "RedDy" MorGan,
>
> tYpoGrAPhiCaL tOuRist.

"May I keep this?" I asked.

"Yes, I reckon. It's the only one I've got, but my printer has the plate, and I'll order some more by telegraph."

The stranger had become quite serious during the latter part of his speech. Giving himself a shake, he once more assumed his careless air, and said:

"Say, boss, will you print a panful for me while I go out to the telegraph office?"

I knew the telegraph office always closed at 7 o'clock, but didn't say so. To his query I replied:

"Go out, if you wish; but don't stay long, as there is a great deal to do, and I hope you'll help us out."

As the door closed behind him I turned to Abe, saying:

"Well, tell me about him. Where did he come from, and how did you happen to get him to work?"

"Shortly after you went away this afternoon he walked into the room and sang out, 'Here I am! Which frame do I take?' I asked him who he was and what he wanted. 'I'm Reddy Morgan,' he said, 'and I've got three medals as champion print, pedestrian and faster. I want a square, and am willing to dis, print, pull the press, swing a brayer or write an editorial to pay for the fodder.' I knew then he was a printer, and as we needed help badly I gave him the meal ticket and sent him down to Steve's telling him to get his dinner, after which, if he would come back, he should have a day's work and be paid in cash for it."

"That was proper; but did he explain why he was in his present fix, or tell where he came from?"

"No. He only said that he had just walked into town about an hour before, and I didn't like to ask him anything. Oh, yes; he inquired who lived in the white frame house on the corner, two blocks down. I suppose he meant Mr. Simpson's place, and so told him. 'Well, your Simpson is a cold-blooded snoozer,' he said. 'I stopped at his back gate, where he was feeding some pretty straight looking grub to a bench-legged dog, and asked him for a handout. He threatened to set the dog on me, and said if I didn't get out of that he'd have me locked up in the calaboose. I didn't seem to move with sufficient celerity to suit his nibs, so he flung a chunk of wood at me, and it caught me right between the shoulders. I'll get even with Simpson, old man; you just turn a rule there.'"

"Let us hope he will," I remarked. "Did he help you out much?"

"Well, I should say so! He was back from his dinner in half an hour, and the way that fellow has been piling up type since is a caution. He didn't want any supper — and I wasn't surprised, for I had glanced at the meal ticket when he came back from dinner. About 8 o'clock he borrowed a quarter from me, saying he wanted to go out and get shaved. I didn't say anything when he came back with all his beard, for his breath beat him in. I guess he's out now paying for his telegram with the rest of that quarter."

"He's a character, Abe, there's no doubt on that score. And I rather like the experience. Have the cub go down and tell Steve to put up a double lunch for tonight, and to make it as good as he can. We may not have such a royal guest soon again, so let's give him a banquet."

Just then "Reddy" entered the room, and it wasn't necessary for him to say he had found the telegraph office closed and another place open. His eyes sparkled and his step was buoyant. He was primed for a big night's work and he did it.

Everything went smoothly, and we got the first side off at 12:30. We got up a long report of the Grassy Creek meeting, the "Specials to *The Star*" were more numerous than usual, and I didn't have to set a line. At 4 o'clock everything was up, enough to fill without using a line of dead ads. — something which had never occurred with us before. Morgan called for a "hump backed rule," and pitched in to make up the first page. When he was ready to lock up he reached for the cigar box filled with quoins.

[Quoins are hard wood wedges made with mathematical correctness in assorted sizes and used for tightening the types when in the "form," so that they can be handled as one piece of metal.]

"You haven't got the most complete plant in the country, boys; but you're better fixed than a shop I struck up in Iowa last week."

"How's that?" asked Abe.

"Why, when I asked for the quoins up there the spider legged rooster they called foreman grabbed a hatchet and rushed out the back door. In two minutes he was back with a limb off of a scrubby oak, which he proceeded to chop and split up into small pieces. As he placed about half a cord of the chunks on the stone beside me, he said: 'Confound it! I'll break that cub's back if he don't quit carrying my plugs home for kindling wood! I split a big lot of bully ones the other day.' Fact, boys."

As soon as the forms were on the old Washington handpress I settled with "Reddy." As I handed him his money he said to me:

"Say, boss, may I roll over on that pile of paper and get a short snooze? I want to take the boat for St. Louis today — it's easy beating them — and I need a little rest."

"Certainly. You may lie down on the paper. But why do you hurry off? Better stay a while with us."

"Can't do it; I've a pressing engagement in St. Louis, and I don't have to work when I've got money. I'll be back this way some day to pay a fellow a grudge I owe him; but I can't stay now. What time will a boat be along?"

I picked up a sheet Abe had just pulled, and after consulting the river news said:

"The *Tom Jasper*, of the Northern line, will be along about noon. That reminds me that I have to be at the wharf when she comes down; so I'll see you."

I stepped into the "sanctum" to write a letter I wanted to send by private messenger on the boat. Ten minutes after, when I passed through the work room, "Reddy" was fast asleep on the pile of paper, despite the racket made by the old press. Across his chest lay a large piece of cardboard, on which he had written, in a hand large enough to attract the attention of the men who worked on the weekly, "Call me when the *Tom Jasper* blows her horn."

I was just finishing my breakfast, at 11:30, when I heard a familiar whistle.

"There's the *Mollie*, and I must run down to her."

When I reached the wharf the *Mollie McPike*, a stern wheeler at that time known to every man, woman and child from St. Louis to Keokuk, was just making a landing. A score or more of persons were on the wharf boat, and standing at one side, with a look of unutterable hatred in his face, was "Reddy" Morgan. He was glaring at a group of half a dozen a few feet away. I followed his gaze, and was made somewhat uneasy to see that the most prominent figure of the group was Mr. Simpson. I remembered "Reddy's" threat, and hurriedly stepped to his side, that I might try to restrain him if he should make any open demonstration of the passion that was so strong within him.

"Well, here you are, my tourist friend; but you are ahead of time."

"Yes; couldn't sleep after 10 o'clock," he muttered, without turning his head. "I was knocking around up town when I heard this tub whistle, and as I don't know their toots like you natives do thought it was my boat. Say, there's my man over there!"

"I see; but I wouldn't make any trouble here if I were you. His wife and little girl are with him, and they would be badly frightened if you attacked him."

"Do you mean to tell me that pretty little yellow headed girl is his child?"

"She is. That is little Millie Simpson, a great favorite with half the people in town," I replied.

"I'm done; that beats me. Boss, maybe you won't believe me, but once I had a little girl like that. She died four years ago last Easter," and the hard look left his face, his clenched hands opened and there were tears in his eyes.

I was saved the painful task of making answer to this sad speech, as the *Mollie* had made fast to the wharf boat, and I turned to respond to a salutation made by the mud clerk, who was an old schoolmate of mine.

In ten minutes the captain cried "All on board!" and those who were going to take passage, including Mr. and Mrs. Simpson and their little girl, hurried across the short staging and up the cabin stairs. The little steamer backed out and down the stream until about sixty yards from the shore, when, with her nose pointed straight at the north pole, her engines were reversed, and she began to move up stream. Just as soon as she got under headway the roustabouts — all darkies — gathered on the forward deck and broke out into that song so familiar to residents of river towns in those days, and sang as only Mississippi river roustabouts could sing. The leader, perched upon some high object of freight, sang the first and third lines as a solo, and the whole crew joined in the others, which were a sort of refrain. One should hear the tune to thoroughly appreciate this musical gem, but here are some of the words:

> A bully boat and captain too;
>   Row, Mollie; row, gal!
> A handsome mate and jolly crew;
>   Row, Mollie row, gal!

Of course the words were always made to suit the particular boat upon which they were being sung.

Mr. and Mrs. Simpson had passed through the cabin and out on to the cabin deck, taking little Millie with them. They had taken a position near the stern of the boat, so that they might see & be seen by their friends on the wharf as long as possible, and were waving their handkerchiefs. As the *Mollie* was just opposite the wharf boat Millie was raised to a standing position on the guard rail by her mother, who passed one arm around the child while employing the other in waving goodbyes.

Suddenly Millie threw out her hands, as if in imitation of her mother. The latter was unprepared for such a movement. The child broke from her light clasp and fell into the river, just far enough from the boat's side to be out of reach of its big wheel's suction. Mrs. Simpson's wild cry was heard high above the beating of the *Mollie*'s wheel and the singing of her jolly crew, and only her husband's strong arm restrained her from plunging madly in after the child. We on the wharf boat saw the little one jump, and the faces that were smiling at her efforts to wave adieu paled, and the mother's anguish had an echo in every heart.

I felt and heard something rush by me, and the old landing dock settled down as if wave-rocked as the figure of a man shot out into the deep water ten feet beyond. He was coatless and bareheaded, and there could be no mistaking, by one who had seen it, that head of bushy hair. It was "Reddy" Morgan. Before the boat's officers knew what was the matter and had rung down her engines "Reddy" was more than half way from the dock to the spot where Millie had first disappeared. The holder of three championship medals should have had one more, for he could swim with a motion as "speedy" as that he used in setting long primer.

"Farther down stream!" shouted a man on the shore. "Reddy" raised his body half out of the water, gave a quick glance off to his right and struck out again. Once more he seemed to stand upright, and then plunge head first under the water. He was down half a minute, which seemed an hour to the anxious watchers, then up he came with a rush as if shot from a spring, and high, on his shoulder was a something which we knew intuitively was the child.

By this time two men in a skiff were pulling from the wharf to "Reddy's" assistance. The *Mollie* had slowed down and was preparing to land. The skiff was soon by "Reddy's" side, and we heard him blurt out, as if short of breath:

"I'll carry the — little one — boys; but you must tow — us in."

He grasped the stern of the small boat as it swung around within reach, and the boatman carefully pulled for a point on the shore just below the wharf boat.

"Give me something to lay her on," said "Reddy," as he hurried out into the gravel beach. In an instant half a dozen coats were spread out upon the beach and the unconscious child was placed upon them. After carefully removing her shoes and stockings and tearing open her dress, Morgan began to roll her about and to slap her back with his open hand. She showed signs of recovering, and the tramp, who seemed to know just what to do, said, "One of you rub her hands and another slap her feet."

He got on to his feet, and, drawing a black bottle from his hip pocket, pulled its cork with his teeth and sat down again. Taking the little girl in his arms he gently forced the mouth of the flask between her lips. She swallowed something with a shudder, and "Reddy" passed the bottle to me and pointed to the cork between his teeth. I understood him. Then he took up one of the dryest coats and wrapped it about the child as she lay in his arms.

"She'll be all right now," he said.

Just then the *Mollie* rubbed against the wharf boat, and a white faced woman ran toward us, followed by half a dozen men, the foremost of whom was her husband.

"My child! My Millie! Where is she?"

"She is here, and is uninjured, Mrs. Simpson," said several at once.

"Reddy" arose easily, and without saying a word gently laid little Millie in her mother's arms. Then he stooped, picked something from the ground and hurriedly thrust it inside his shirt. I alone observed this movement as I handed him his bottle, saying, "You had better take some of this stuff yourself, old man."

"Not now," he replied, and put the bottle in his pocket. As he turned to move away Mr. Simpson came up to him, and speaking with considerable emotion said:

"My good man, I am your debtor for more than I can ever pay. What can I say. What can I do to in part show how deeply grateful I am?"

"Nothing!" answered "Reddy" rather crossly, and without changing his position.

"But, sir, I insist. You do not look like one who has all he could use of this world's goods. I hope you will accept a small token of my gratitude," and Mr. Simpson took from his wallet a twenty-dollar bill and held it out.

"I'll take nothing from you. As you say, I am not overburdened with worldly goods, and I've seen the time — and not long ago — when I didn't have a cent and was hungry; but I don't want any of your money. I'd advise you to take that sawbuck and buy new padlocks for the calaboose with it."

"Reddy" turned, and the man who had treated him so unfeelingly twenty-four hours before saw to whom he was indebted for saving his child's life. His face flushed and he looked very uncomfortable, but he said:

"I was hasty yesterday, my good man, and I ask your forgiveness, I promise you that no man shall again be turned away from my door hungry. Pardon the wrong I did you, and accept something from me for the service you have done me and mine today."

"No," said "Reddy" in a softer tone than his former abrupt refusal. "I'm willing to call it even, and let bygones be bygones, but all the reward I want for bringing the little girl out I've got here," and he placed his hand upon his breast.

Every one present, excepting myself, thought he referred only to a consciousness of a duty done; but I had not forgotten his act of secreting something between his shirt and that breast as I stepped up to return his flask. I knew his words had other meaning. He went over to the wharf boat, picked up his coat, and putting it on as he walked, passed up the levee toward the business part of town.

Mr. Simpson, with a grieved look on his face, turned away and joined his wife and friends. Millie was smiling as she lay in her mother's arms. She needed only dry clothing and a little care, to avoid a cold, to be in a few hours as well as she ever was. The trip up the river had been abandoned for that day, so far as the Simpson family was concerned. The little girl's hat, shoes and other articles of apparel which had been removed were gathered up, all but one little stocking. That could not be found. I knew where it was and so did "Reddy;" but I kept his secret.

The *Mollie* had once more started up the stream, but there was no singing this time. The superstitious darkies were dumb for the time being. In a few minutes all the women and most of the men had left the wharf. About a score of young men still lingered near the old dock talking. One of them, who had overheard the conversation between Mr. Simpson and "Reddy," asked if any one knew the meaning of it. I gave a partial explanation, and then it was proposed that we make up a purse right there for the brave fellow. A collection was at once taken, and a sum which more than equaled Mr. Simpson's "sawbuck" was the result.

We hurried off to find our man, and soon learned that he had gone into Steve's. Yes, there he was — in the kitchen, sitting as close as he could get to the big cook stove, and steaming like a Broadway manhole with the cover off.

"Morgan," I said, "I have given your admirers here an idea of why you refused to accept anything from Mr. Simpson, and they have made up this little purse for you, and we all hope you will accept it."

"You heard me say I didn't want to be paid for what any square man who could swim would do."

"Yes, we heard you; but listen to me," and I stepped close to him and whispered, "I know what you've got inside your shirt; I saw you pick it up. Shall I tell the boys, or will you take the purse?"

He put one hand over my mouth, and jumping quickly to his feet said:

"Friends, I'll take it. I still think you overestimate what I did, but you mean well and I like you for it. If I didn't have to be continually traveling on account of my health I'd stay here and be elected mayor, so that I could tear down that old calaboose or turn it into a soup house. But, jokes aside, I want to ask one thing of you, friends. Don't be too hard on the tramp. They're not all like me; I'm one from choice. But in the last two or three years many a good man has been forced on to the road. There's a great big world outside of your quiet little town, and there's a good deal of hardship and misery in it. Lots of poor devils are trying to get away from it, and they keep walking and walking. When a seedy looking stranger strikes you for a lift don't be in a hurry to refuse him. Find out if it wasn't want of work that pulled him down, and his unsuccessful hunt for it that made him seedy."

There was perfect quiet in the little restaurant for a moment, then some one proposed "three cheers for 'Reddy' Morgan," which were heartily given, and all filed out.

An hour later the *Tom Jasper* touched at the old wharf boat, two hours behind time. As she steamed away down the river one of her passengers was a hero and the first tramp printer I ever saw.

I never met him again, but do not think I shall ever forget him. While overhauling some old papers today the grotesque card of the "Typographical Tourist" met my gaze, and the events which I have tried to relate in the foregoing passed before my mind as distinctly as if they had happened only yesterday.

Greeley's Handwriting

I HAD NEVER KNOWN a tramp printer of sufficient age who had not worked on the New York *Tribune* in the Greeley days, and who did not, consequently, have reminiscences of the great editor's copy. With this fact in mind one evening, when old Mark Wallis, my compositor, was sober, and therefore in a colloquial mood, I gently led up to the subject.

"Yes," he said, with the utmost confidence, "I was on the *Tribune* for a year in the early sixties. I never saw much of Greeley's copy, as that was mostly set by one man, a hoary-headed anachronism who smoked a cob pipe with the corn still on it. He boasted that he could read Greeley's copy at three yards with one eye shut. Tangled and terrible as it was, it was said to be really less difficult to read when taken in detail than you might suppose, much of its bad reputation having sprung from the horror inspired in surveying a page of it as a whole. But whether difficult or not, there were few errors made in setting it. I never knew of an instance in the *Tribune* office like the one I once met with in a small Ohio town, where the editor was one week obliged to put this on his first page, after his second and third had been printed: ☞ ERRATUM: For 'Price of Nails,' in the foreign editorial on our inside, read 'Prince of Wales.'

"This man of the agricultural pipe, who was named Larkway, and who, I hope in the interest of archaeology, has been preserved in some museum, was so much given to bragging about his ability to read Greeley's copy that he was a burden to the office. There came to be a tacit understanding that an attempt must be made to humble him; but when the attempt was made it was practically a failure.

"Mr. Greeley was constantly receiving offerings of the products of the earth from rural admirers, as if he were a sort of modern Ceres and the *Tribune* office his temple. Sometimes it would be a big melon; again a prize squash; on another occasion a champion pumpkin. From the choice ears of corn which he got, Larkway used to make his pipes. Often he would not even remove the husks, and on one occasion these caught fire as he was studying an obscure word, and gained considerable headway before he noticed it. Sometimes an aspiring country boy would send Mr. Greeley a whistle made out of a pig's tail, just to show that it could be done, despite the popular belief to the contrary; and Larkway would take one of these, bore a hole through it, and use it for a stem to his pipe, thus getting, in a crude form, along with his tobacco, that Southern staple, hog and hominy.

"One day a worshipper in Herkimer County sacrificed on the Greeley altar two young roosters, alive. They were of a new strain, originated by the man, and he had named it the Go-West breed. Mr. Greeley was much interested in the new fowls, and gave the man a good notice in the agricultural department, and cooped them under his desk, bestowing upon them an old straw hat for their brooding-place, since they were not large enough to roost.

"In fact, the man, in his eagerness to pour out his feathery libation, had sent these cockerels when they could not have been over a month old. They were so young that they required soft food, so Greeley used to bring down corn meal and mix it up with water for them. This pabulum, together with the cockroaches, which they soon learned to run to earth, constituted their diet, and they prospered and grew. But they had not been in the office a fortnight before they developed a trick which brought them into disfavor. They learned to eat the paste. They would hop up on their owner's desk and gorge themselves from the paste-pot as regularly as he went out, seldom leaving enough to stick a gumless postage-stamp.

"It was a favorite plan of Greeley's to clip an item from a loathed contemporary, paste it on the top of a sheet of copy paper, and then proceeded to tear the unfortunate author of the paragraph limb from limb, beginning with the truculent, 'You lie, you villain, you lie!' and ending with the crushing, 'We don't want to hear from you again.' Several times, when boiling with rage at something he had just clipped, he started to dab it on a piece of paper, and found the paste-pot polished out like a lamp chimney, and saw those two roosters standing about in a calm attitude almost ready to burst. He endured it a week for the sake of the breed, but it happened once too often, and Greeley was the one who burst. He sent for the foreman, and said to him:

"'Do you see those two confounded young roosters? They've eaten up my paste. They're full of it. They're waiting for me to get some more. I want you to take 'em up stairs, and never let me see 'em again.'

"The foreman tucked a rooster under either arm, and did as he was told; and thus they came to make their home in the composing-room.

"Here they continued to prosper, getting plenty of cockroaches and corn meal, with an occasional snatch at the foreman's paste-pot; and once in a while the galley-boy used to give them a mouthful of news ink on the end of a column rule, which seemed to agree with them, though this, or something else, had a bad effect on their tempers, and they began to fight each other a good deal. They constantly grew more combative, until it seemed that, instead of being called the Go-Wests, a more appropriate name would have been the On-to-Richmonds.

"After they had been with us a couple of weeks the boy one day left the ink-roller of the proof-press on the floor. One of the roosters walked over it, and then across a piece of white paper.

The foreman saw him, and a great light burst in upon his mind, which nearly stunned him. He slapped his leg with his hand hard enough to break it, and shut his jaws together like a vise to keep from breaking out in a volcano of laughter. He walked to his desk as if in a trance, keeping his eye on Larkway. Before he went home he spoke to the proof-reader and one or two others, and they near fractured their legs with their hands.

"The next afternoon they were back at the office two hours before the usual time. The foreman caught one rooster and the proof-reader the other, and they took them over in the corner behind the imposing-stones. They had previously sent the devil down to Mr. Greeley's room to get a dozen sheets of the paper he always wrote on. These they spread on the floor in the form of a square, carefully inked the feet of the fowls, and set them to fighting on the copy paper. They had just had a meal of cockroaches, and they went at each other savagely. Every two or three minutes the men would take them off, ink the bottoms of their feet, and toss them into the ring again. At the end of twenty minutes every sheet of the paper was covered with their tracks, and the foreman gathered up the pages, numbered them, and scrawled a head on the first one, *The Plain Duty of Congress*, in imitation of Greeley's hand, marked the whole 'Brevier Double Lead,' and hung it on the copy-hook.

"Pretty soon the men began to drop in, but they had all heard of the game that was on, and picked around the article. After a while Larkway came lumbering along. He had just made a new pipe out of the biggest ear of corn ever raised in Cayuga County, and a particularly crooked pig's tail from Brattleboro, Vermont, and seemed unusually pert. He started the conflagration in his pipe, put on his spectacles, and walked to the hook.

"'Hey? You fellers still soldiering, ain't you?' he cried. 'Still afraid of the old man's stuff, hey? Can't rastle it, can you? Had to leave it for old Larkway, didn't you? Well, that's all right; I like it. You do me a favor when you leave it for me.'

"He took it, walked over and slammed it down on his upper case, planted a handful of leads on the bottom of it, and picked up his stick. Every man in the room held his sides, and watched to see the old fossil flabbergasted; but, by the Goddess of Truth, he began to set it!

"Yes, Larkway started to set it. At the end of the second line he began to look a little troubled, laid down his stick, and we thought our moment of victory was come; but he only swore a little, knocked the ashes out of his pipe, refilled it, lit it with a husk stripped from the outside, picked up his stick, and went on. You could have packed every one of us in a hat-box. The old cave-dweller worked on, and never looked up again until he got almost to the bottom of the last page. Here he stuck, on a place where one of the roosters had slapped down the edge of his wing, also inky. Larkway studied over it for a long time, then he said to the foreman: 'Darn it, the best of us get hung up on a word once in a while. What's that, down there?' 'Don't ask me,' said the foreman. 'You know I can't read the stuff. Go down and ask the old man himself.'

"Larkway shuffled out with a long face, carrying his pipe in one hand and the copy in the other. He went into the chief's room, and said, in a low tone. 'Mr. Greeley, I'm stuck. What is that word?'

"Greeley snatched the sheet from his hand impatiently, studied it a moment, and then squeaked, in his highest voice: '"Unconstitutional," sir! Great Jehoshaphat! it seems to me sometimes as if this office was full of pesky college graduates, and after I've given the janitor strict orders not to allow one of 'em in the building!'"

The Old-Time Printer

THE PICTURESQUE "PANHANDLING" old-time typographical chronic tourist has passed, and in his stead has come to stay the product of the Linotype period — the well dressed, well fed, prosperous disciple of Gutenberg — and of Mergenthaler — who is anything save a migratory being.

The old-time "tramp" printer needed no overcoat, for, like the birds of the air that seek the sunshine at all seasons of the year, the panhandling tourist of old abided in New Orleans in winter and in St. Paul in summer.

He was a jovial, carefree individual, and the average "tourist" could set more type and cleaner proof than the hand typesetter who looked upon him as an inferior member of the craft.

I shall dwell upon just a few of the celebrities who walked, or hit the "blind baggage" in ye olden time; and when "subs" were scarce, as they generally were in those days, they were welcome visitors in the offices of the smaller daily newspapers of the country.

"ROCKY MOUNTAIN" SMITH.

While I was "cub" on the Burlington *Hawkeye* and setting solid brevier about 2 o'clock one morning, there appeared in the doorway of the newsroom, unheralded, a gaunt specimen of the genus "tramp," whom I afterward learned bore the so-briquet "Rocky Mountain" Smith. It was nearing "closing up" time and the *Hawkeye* force was plugging away hard; silence reigning save for the clicking of the type. In dramatic voice the apparition in the doorway said:

> Up stepped ye gallant printer man, and boldly came to taw:
> Says he, "You'll have to spill some blood before you touch a squaw."
> What keered that crowd for printer man? They didn't care three straws,
> Just busted into that there hut, and hustled out the squaws.
> Then louder rang the pans and cans, and louder the huzzahs,
> And nothing more was ever heard of those unprotected squaws.

> **MORAL:**
> I'd rather be a little bird, beneath some grizzly's paws
> Than take the desperate chances of those unprotected squaws.

"How's work, fellows?"

Smith remained in Burlington a couple of weeks and departed south on a raft, bound for St. Louis.

"LIGHTNING TYPESETTER."

To the "cub" in a newspaper office such characters as "Rocky Mountain" Smith were a revelation. Shortly after the departure of Smith there came into the *Hawkeye* office another celebrated tourist, Tom Walker, known as "The Lightning Typesetter of the West."

Walker had walked some 30 miles that day, so he said, and was too footsore and weary to work. He ranked me as "a likely looking kid" and "panhandled" me for half a dollar. The reader will now understand the meaning of "panhandling."

This tourist remained with us only a few days. He worked a couple of nights and his average "string" was a couple of thousand a night more than that of any of the regulars on the *Hawkeye*.

CHURCH AND STEIN.

These two worthies of the road came in after Walker and remained several weeks. And the way they could set type was a

caution. They made no fuss about it, either, but each morning Church and Stein hung strings on the hook that made the
"cub" wonder how much type they could have set if they had refrained from taking an occasional smoke during composition
hours, for they would scrape their pipes, load up and sit by the
big cannon stove while they smoked.

One day Church and Stein disappeared, and they were not
seen again until about the same time the following year.

"SID" BENNETT APPEARS.

"Sid" Bennett was about the best-dressed panhandler the "cub"
had ever seen. He was tall and well built, straight as an ar-
row, wore good clothes, always black and of the latest cut. His
beard and mustache were black and always neatly trimmed.
He was dignified to a degree and might have been mistaken for
a supreme court justice. Yet "Sid" was a professional "tramp"
printer and panhandler.

It was related in those days that during the Centennial in
Philadelphia, in 1876, "Sid" was left in charge of a weekly newspaper office in Nebraska while the proprietor attended the
Centennial. During the absence of the proprietor a "prospec-
tor" came along and wanted to buy the paper. "Sid" sold it to
him, took a small earnest fee and departed. Just what the proprietor said when he returned is not known.

One night when the types that made the *Hawkeye* were
clicking into the sticks there walked into the office as fine a
specimen of an athlete as the "cub" had ever seen. Tall, broad
shouldered, of massive frame, this tourist appeared a physical
master of men. His name proved to be Jack Curly, and legend
says that on one occasion when Charley Gallagher was slated
to meet another gladiator of the ring near New Orleans and
Gallagher's opponent failed to appear, Curly stripped off his
coat and took on Gallagher, as he put it, "Rather than see the
crowd at the fight disappointed."

When Curly wanted to work he would say so, and he worked whether the regular wanted to lay off or not. Like the others, he was a fine printer.

One day while Curly was in Burlington, Andy Hughes came to town. Hughes was another noted panhandler. Curly did not like Hughes, and informed Andy that one town was too small to contain both at the same time, and as he liked Burlington Hughes would have to go. Andy left that night — on a raft.

"HIGH HAND" ARRIVES.

"High Hand," as he signed it, was presumed to be Hiram Hahn. He had tramped from Maine to California, and back again, several times. He was an excellent compositor, rapid and correct, and a makeup to boot.

"High" considered it a crime to work more than two days a week, hence his panhandling was oftener practiced than by the ordinary tourist.

Bill Mason was another of the old timers whose speed at the case was marvelous. Bill, like "High," was averse to long hours and prolonged days. The pair met in Burlington and left together with the avowed intention of walking from Burlington to New York.

Whether they walked or took "blind baggage" will never be known, but they reached the metropolis in due season, and wrote back that it was a great village.

SENECA TRUESDELL'S BAD BREAK.

Along about the time that Bob Burdette, now the Rev. Robert J. Burdette of Los Angeles, was making fame on the Burlington *Hawkeye* as a humorist, C. Y. Wheeler was business manager of that newspaper. Wheeler was ranked by the force as "stingy." It was a nightly occurrence to see typesetters on the *Hawkeye* stop and "pick leads." The supply was short.

Seneca Truesdell, a St. Paul tourist, was subbing on the *Hawk-*

eye and kicking consistently on "pulling leads" with "phat" on the hook, for in those days even a bit of leaded brevier was some "phat."

Seneca was witty. Manager Wheeler was in the newsroom one afternoon, talking with foreman Tom Donahue. Seneca saw his opportunity, and said to one of the regulars:

"Going over to Biggsville Sunday?"

Biggsville was a hamlet containing some half a dozen houses, and no newspaper office.

"Maybe," was the response. "Why?"

"Well. If you do," replied Seneca, "just scamper around and see if you can dig up a handful of leads."

Wheeler "saw the joke" and ordered Seneca "fired."

WHEELER AND BURDETTE.

Just how true the story is, Bob Burdette may tell, but it was related in those days that Wheeler went to Peoria, Burdette's home at that time, and sought to sign up the humorist for the *Hawkeye*. While he had caught Truesdell's affront he was not quick to appreciate real humor, and was nonplused when Burdette is said to have stated that he would like a job on the *Hawkeye* were it not for the fact that certain people in Peoria might object to his leaving that town.

"Well, let's see them and find out," said Wheeler. "Who shall we see first?"

"I would suggest the sheriff," replied Bob, with a merry twinkle in those keen black eyes. "He knows how much I owe."

Whatever it was it was paid, and Burdette became a part of the *Hawkeye* force.

Bob Burdette

How Bob Burdette Writes

BURDETTE does the most of his writing on the cars, and his manuscript is something between the Choctaw language and the hieroglyphics on the Egyptian obelisks. He says of it: "When I first got at it the printers would draw cuts for my copy, and those who got a slice of it would go around trying to hire a boy to kick them down stairs and break their necks. However, there was one old fellow who thirsted after it, and when he got a piece of it he immediately put on a 'sub' and went on a drunk. Under any other circumstances he would have been discharged. I do better now. I had to, because it had almost broken up the Printers' Temperance Union. The patrons of the cause in Burlington traced the thing back to me, and I had to improve my copy. It didn't hurt me much but it was a thundering blow to the printers." — *Oil City Derrick*, 1881

ROBERT J. BURDETTE (1844–1914), born in Pennsylvania, was known as "The Man of the Burlington [Iowa] *Hawkeye*." During the Civil War he was a private in the 47th Illinois infantry. In 1869 he became night editor of the *Peoria Daily Transcript* and was associated with many papers after that. His humorous paragraphs were picked up as "Exchanges" (like that above) and run by many papers throughout the country. He went on the lecture circuit with a talk titled "The Rise and Fall of the Mustache," which he delivered 3000 times during 30 years. In 1897 he became a Baptist minister and moved to Los Angeles where he married and settled in Pasadena.

The Old Printer.

HE WAS SHORT OF TYPE AND WHEN "30" CAME,
HIS SPIRIT HAD FLOWN.*

AND SO, YEAR AFTER YEAR, he wrought among the boys on a morning paper. He went to bed about the time the rest of the world got up, and he arose about the time the rest of the world sat down to dinner. He worked by every kind of light except sunlight. There were candles in the office when he came in; then they had lard oil lamps that smoked and sputtered and smelled; then he saw two or three printers blinded by explosions of camphene and spirit gas; then kerosene came in and heated up the newsrooms on summer nights like a furnace; then the office put in gas, and now the electric light swung from the ceiling and dazzled his old eyes and glared into them from his copy.

---

* Thirty is the printer's term for "there is no more," because of the three 'X's marked at the end of a manuscript so the typesetter knows the text is finished.

If he sang on his way home a policeman bade him "cheese that," and reminded him that he was disturbing the peace and people wanted to sleep. But when he wanted to sleep, the rest of the world, for whom he has sat up all night to make a morning paper, roared and crashed by down the noisy streets under his window, with cart and truck and omnibus; blared out with brass bands, howled with hand organs, talked and shouted, and even the shrieking newsboys, with a ghastly sarcasm, murdered the sleep of the tired old printer by yelling the name of his own paper.

Year after year the foreman roared at him to remember that this was not an afternoon paper, editors shrieked down the tube to have a blind man put on that dead man's case, smart young proof-readers scribbled sarcastic comments on his work on the margin of his proof slips that they didn't know how to read, long winded correspondents learning to write and long haired poets who could never learn to spell wrathfully cast all their imperfections upon his head. But through it all he wrought patiently and found more sunshine than shadow in the world; he had more friends than enemies.

Printers and foremen and pressmen and reporters and editors came and went, but he staid, and he saw newspapers and sanctum filled and emptied and filled and emptied again, and filled with new strange faces. He believed in his craft, and to the end he had a silent pity, that came as near being contempt as his good, forgiving old heart could feel, for an editor who had not worked his way from a regular devil-ship up past the cases and the imposing stone. He worked all that night, and when the hours that are so short in the ball-room and so long in the composing-room drew wearily on, he was tired. He hadn't thrown in a very full case, he said, and he had to climb clear into the boxes and chase a type up into a corner before he could get hold of it. One of the boys, tired as himself — but a printer is never too tired to be good-natured — offered to change places with him, but the old man said there was enough in the case to last him through this take, and he wouldn't work any more to-night. The type clicked in the silent room, and by and by the old man said:

"I'm out of sorts."

And he sat down on the low window sill by his case, with his stick in his hand, his hands folded wearily in his lap. The types clicked on. A galley of telegraph waited.

"What gentleman is lingering with 13D?" called the foreman, who was dangerously polished and polite when he was on the point of exploding with wrath and importance. Slug 9, passing by the alley, stopped to speak to the old man sitting there so quietly. The telegraph boy came running in with the last manifold sheet, shouting:

"Thirty!"

They carried the old man to the foreman's long table and laid him down reverently and covered his face. They took the stick out of his nerveless hand and read his last take:

BOSTON, Nov. 23.— The American bark *Pilgrim* went to pieces off Marblehead in a light gale about midnight. She was old and unseaworthy, and this was to have been her last trip.

Bibliography

Adams, William E., *Memoirs of a Social Atom*, London: Hutcheson & Co., 1903; reprinted New York: Augustus M. Kelley, 1967

Bakhtin, Mikhail, *Rabelais and his World*, Indiana University Press, 1984

Boutin, Otto J., *A Catfish in the Bodoni*, St. Cloud: North Star Press, 1970

Cubery, William M., *Fifty Years a Printer*, San Francisco: Cubery, 1900

Duffy, Patrick, *The Skilled Compositor, 1850–1914. An Aristocrat among Working Men*, Aldershot: Ashgate, 2000

Gent, Thomas, *The Life of Mr Thomas Gent, Printer of York, Written by Himself*, London: Printed for Thomas Thorpe, 1832

Gordon, John, *A Memorial to the Tramp Printer*, South Brewer, Maine: The Gordon Press, 1927

Graham, J. B., *Handset Reminiscences*, Salt Lake City: Century Printing Company, 1915

Greeley, Horace, *Recollections of a Busy Life*, New York: J. B. Ford, 1868

Harte, Bret, *Stories and Poems, and Other Uncollected Writings*, edited by Charles Meeker Kozlay, volume 20, Boston: Houghton-Mifflin, 1914

Hicks, John Edward, *Adventures of a Tramp Printer, 1880–1890*, Kansas City: MidAmericana Press, 1950

Hobsbawm, E. J., "The Tramping Artisan" in *The Economic History Review*, Second Series, vol. III, no. 3, 1951, pp. 299–320

Howells, John & Marion Dearman, *Tramp Printers*, Pacific Grove, California: Discovery Press, 1996

Johnston, Alastair M., *Alphabets to Order: The Literature of Nineteenth-Century Typefounders' Specimens*, The British Library & Oak Knoll Press, 2000

Lampman, Ben Hur, *The Tramp Printer. Sometime Journeyman of the Little Home-Town Papers in Days that Come No More*, Portland, Oregon: Metropolitan Press, 1934

Levenson, Roger, *Women in Printing, Northern California 1857–90*, Santa Barbara: Capra Press, 1994

Nye, Bill, *Remarks*, Chicago: A. E. Davis & Co., 1887

Pretzer, William S., "Tramp Printers. Craft Culture, Trade Unions and Technology," in *Printing History* (Journal of the American Printing History Association), vol. 6, no. 2, 1984

Quad, M. [C. B. Lewis], *Quad's Odds*, Detroit: R. D. S. Tyler & Co., 1875

Read, Opie, *Old Ebenezer*, Chicago: Laird & Lee, 1897

Rounds, Sterling F., *Among the Craft. Notes by the Way*, edited by James Eckman, New York: Typophiles, 1970

Rounsfell, J. W., *On the Road, Journeys of a Tramping Printer*, edited by Andrew Whitehead, Horsham, Sussex: Caliban Books, 1982

Rumble, Walker, *The Swifts. Printers in the Age of Typesetting Races*, University of Virginia Press, 2003

Saum, Lewis O., *Eugene Field & his Age*, University of Nebraska Press, 2001

Smith, Charles Manby, *The Working Man's Way in the World*, London: W. & F. G. Cash, 1857; reprinted London: Printing Historical Society 1967

Smith, Harriet E., ed., *Autobiography of Mark Twain*, volume 1, University of California Press, 2010

Visscher, William Lightfoot, L.L.B. *Vissch. Credited to Matthew Mattox, N.P.R.*, Saint Joseph, Missouri: J. B. Johnson, 1873

Webb, Sidney and Beatrice, *Industrial Democracy*, London: Longmans, Green & Co., 1897; reprinted 1920; and New York: A. M. Kelley, 1965

Williams, Robert, *The Chicago Diaries of John M. Wing 1865–6*, Southern Illinois University Press, 2002

This book is set in Miller Text with display in Franklin Gothic. Headers were created with "Artistic Printing" ornaments from the 1880s and repros of type from the Poltroon Press collection. The devil dingbat is from the 1888 Cincinnati Typefoundry specimen; the train, bath, dog & Acorn press cuts come from the Elrie Robinson collection at New York Public Library; the other cuts and combination border ornaments come from MacKellar, Smiths & Jordan's 1882 book. The cover ornaments are from a Frederic Wesselhoeft advertisement in *The British Printer* from November 1889.